Simple & Useful:
A Guide to Web Design

Jerrold Maddox
The Pennsylvania State University

"one web for anyone, everywhere, on anything"
-Tim Berners-Lee

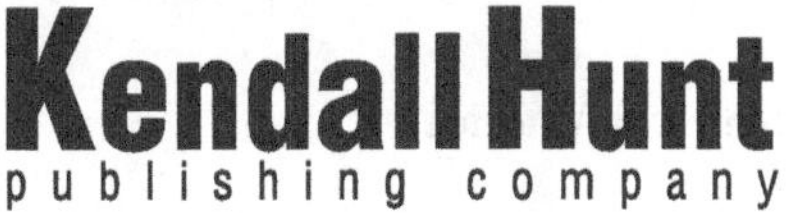

Cover image © Shutterstock, Inc.

Kendall Hunt
publishing company

www.kendallhunt.com
Send all inquiries to:
4050 Westmark Drive
Dubuque, IA 52004-1840

ISBN 978-1-4652-1939-8

Printed in the United States of America
10 9 8 7 6 5 4 3 2

One of the fundamental properties of the web is the fact that it is just one space, and it's a consensual space. It should be independent of the hardware you use. It should be independent of the software you use or the operating system it's running on. It should also be independent of what culture you're in, or whether you're writing a wonderful, carefully edited document, or whether you're scribbling something on the back of the proverbial envelope. And it should be independent of what language you're using, what character set, whether your letters go up and down, left to right, or right to left. Also, people should be able to access that information even if they have disabilities. At W3C we call this concept "one web for anyone, everywhere, on anything."

–Tim Berners-Lee
MIT Technology Review by
Mark Frauenfelder, October 1, 2004.

CONTENTS

Introduction

This is question that led to this book:

Can html be styled well enough and simply enough so that anyone can write for the web, using just a text editor, and share that work with anyone else, regardless of the platform he or she is using, the speed of the connection and any disabilities he or she may have?

The answer is yes.

I also believe that those of us who are focused on teaching and learning, rather than branding and sales, need to make everything as simple and small as we can, so we don't burden the user who has limited bandwidth and a slow connection.

In that way, we make the web more accessible and easier to use for everyone.

It starts with the basics: what needs to be included in your markup so your work will scale to all devices – from phones to being projected on to a screen – and be available to the disabled: physically, intellectually, and emotionally.

To do that, some simple rules need to be followed such as using correct tags in html5 and in css3.

Working is this way also saves time and labor, and, since it does not ask for the skills required to do complex scripting or media-rich websites, it puts doing web work within everyone's reach.

First, it is necessary to look closely at what information you want to present and ask if it will be available to those whose connection to the Internet is 3 Mbps or less. Do your files exceed 100k? If so, why? Could the information be presented just as well in a format that downloads quickly? In that way you will keep the user's attention on your site; most leave a site if it takes more than 5 seconds to load.

The best format is usually text, since it takes the least space. For instance, if a photograph is 40 k in size, that equals about 3000 words of text, or a dozen type-written pages (1 second of video is about 4 Mb, over 4000 k or 1200 typewritten pages), and text is also simple and easy to enter, to correct, and to update.

Text is, as well, the easiest medium to translate into an accessible form for the disabled.

Since most of the information on the web is in text, making it easy to read is central to this book. Areas of discussion include the choice of words, the length of sentences and paragraphs, the selection of fonts and their size, and the length of the lines of text and the spaces between them.

Writing your web pages can be done with text editor, like TextEdit on a Mac or NotePad on a PC. There are also free html editors; TextWrangler and Komodo are two excellent ones.

Basics

These five lines are essential to any site that is going work on all devices and be accessible; every page should to begin with them.

```
<!doctype html>
<html lang=en>
<head>
<meta charset=utf-8>
<meta name=viewport content="width=device-width,user-scalable=yes">
```

Each matters because it tells the browser what it should do with this document because:

1 – It is html `(!doctype html)`.
2 –The primary language is English `(lang=en)`.
3 – It works with a multi-language character set `(charset=utf-8)`.
4 – It scales to the device it is on `(viewport content="width=device-width,user-scalable=yes)`.

`lang=en` may be changed if the site is in another language, so a text-to-speech reader would know how to pronounce the words.

Here are the HTML5 tags that are most frequently used within the `<body>`. These tags help give your pages a meaningful structure so they can be navigated by a machine reader or someone using a screen reader.

```
<header>
<hgroup>
<nav>
<article>
<section>
<figure>
<figcaption>
<aside>
<footer>
```

Navigation

When you design the navigation for your site, make sure the font is large enough and that the contrast is strong enough to be easily seen. Too often the site navigation is done like this:

Registration | Curriculum | Students | Parents | Calendar | CampusMap

```
font-size:11px;font-style:italic;color:#ccc;background-color:#777
```

Instead of this:

Registration Curriculum Students Parents Calendar CampusMap

```
font-size:16px;color:#fff;background-color:#000
```

Links

There are absolute links, relative links, email links, and links to navigate within a site.

The absolute link uses the complete url of the site linked to; the relative link uses the relationship to file to which it is linked, whether it is in the same directory or another one within a directory containing the different ones. The email link has mailto and address added, and the link within a site use a # and id. These can take you to a particular place on the current page or to one on another page.

This is what they look like in the markup.

An absolute link:

```
<a href="http://www.psu.edu/">Penn State</a>
```

A relative link:

```
<a href="assignment2.html/">Assignment 2</a>
```

An email link:

```
<a href="mailto:elizabeth@foo.edu">Elizabeth Regina</a>
```

A link within site:

```
<a href="#three">Section 3</a>

<h3 id="three">Section 3</h3>
```

Files and How Their Size Is Measured

These are the most commonly seen units for file size on a computer and the relationship in size they have to each other.

1024 Bytes = 1 Kilobyte
1024 Kilobytes = 1 Megabyte
1024 Megabytes = 1 Gigabyte
1024 Gigabytes = 1 Terabyte

They are also referred to with these abbreviations:

Bytes = B
Kilobytes = KB
Megabytes = MB
Gigabytes = GB
Terabytes = TB

To give an idea of what these units mean: One word equals about 10 B, 10 KB equals a page from a book, a 500-page book in plain text is about 1 MB, the same size as 6 seconds of an uncompressed audio file. 1 GB is around seven minutes of HDTV video or 1000 books, and 1 TB equals the amount of data in a university research library.

The size of your files is especially important if your audience is using a phone or has a slow connection to access the material. As I will point out often, text is, as you can see, the most efficient way to share information. It is also the easiest to use.

Making Images Scale on Different Devices

If you use images and want them to scale on different devices, add this to your style sheet: `img{width:100%;height:auto}`. The % can be varied.

And this in the body: <img src="foo.jpg"alt="foo">

Color

If you use color in your website and set it in your style sheet, use `{color:#930; background-color:#ffe;}`

Instead of color names like `lightslategray` or `goldenrod`, use hex, rgb, or hsl colors.For instance, use one of these color codes: hex `(#daa520)`, rgb `(218,165,32)`, or hsl `(0.12% 0.73% 0.5%)` in place of the color name goldenrod.

If you use color codes, then you can easily make changes, like `#78d` to the hex for `lightslategray(#789)` to make it lighter and more of a blue gray.

This flexibility is especially important when a site will be projected and needs to be edited depending on a specific situation.

HTML5 Elements and Structure

This is a screen shot of the top of the basic site used in this outline that makes concrete the parts of HTML5 and CSS3 outlined in other chapters in this book.

Title

Author

Lorem · Praesent venenatis · At vero

Lorem ipsum dolor sit amet

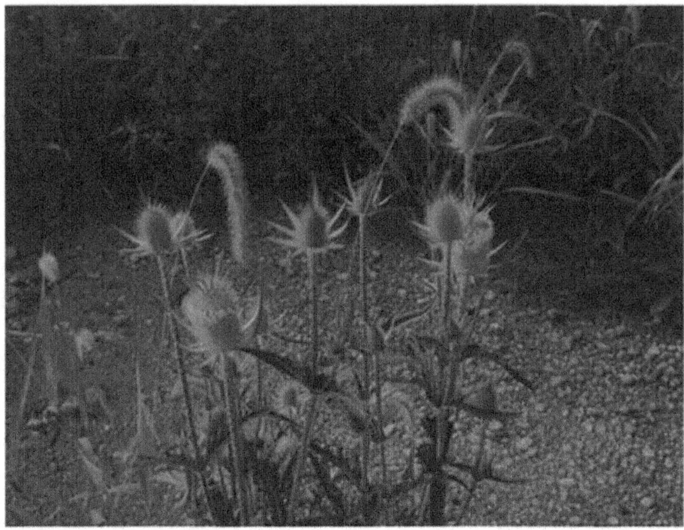

Thistles and timothy, 2010

Lorem ipsum dolor sit amet, consectetur adipiscing elit. Aliquam lobortis enim et lectus dapibus adipiscing. Cum sociis natoque penatibus et magnis dis parturient montes, nascetur ridiculus mus. In id magna elit. Nulla id enim non lacus mollis sollicitudin non quis velit.

This Is the Source of the Page with Shortened Texts:

```
<!DOCTYPE HTML>
<html lang=en>
<head>
<meta name=viewport content="width=device-width,user-scalable=yes">
<link href='http://fonts.googleapis.com/css?family=Droid+Serif:400,
700,400italic,700italic' rel='stylesheet' type='text/css'>
<style type="text/css">
body{margin:0 auto;max-width:33em;word-spacing:.01em;
font-family:"droid serif",georgia, serif;}
html{padding:0 .5em 2em 1em;}
h1{font-size:125%;font-weight:700;
padding:0;letter-spacing:0.12em;margin:1em 0 0 0}
h2{font-size:120%;font-weight:700}
h3{font-size:110%;font-weight:700;}
h4{font-size:105%;font-weight:700}
p{font-size:100%;line-height:1.4em;}
pre{font-size:85%;line-height:1.3em;font-family:"droid sans
mono";line-height:1.4em;max-width:33em}
.mono{max-width:10em}
a:link{color:#831;text-decoration:none}
a:visited {color:#831;text-decoration:none}
img{width:100%;height:auto}
figure {margin:0;}
figcaption{margin: 1em 0;font-size:80%}
blockquote{font-size:95%;line-height:1.4em}
aside{font-size:90%;font-style:italic;margin-left:2em}
</style>
<link rel="stylesheet" type="text/css" href="print.css"
media="print">
<title>Lorem ipsum</title>
</head>
<body>
<header>
<hgroup>
<h1>Title</h1>
<h2>Author</h2>
</hgroup>
<h4><nav><a href="#lorem">Lorem</a> &#183;<a href="#sed"> Praesent
venenatis </a>&#183; <a href="#at">At vero</a></nav></h4>
</header>
<article>
```

```
<section>
<h3 id="lorem">Lorem ipsum dolor sit amet</a></h3>
<figure>
<img src="thistlestimothy.jpg"alt="Thistles and timothy, 2010">
<figcaption> <cite>Thistles and timothy</cite>, 2010</figcaption>
</figure>
<p>Lorem ipsum dolor sit amet, consectetur... </p>
<aside>
<p id=#aside>This is a common fill text. It is in Latin and comes
from Cicero.</p>
</aside>
</section>
<section>
<h3 id="sed">Praesent venenatis dolor</a></h3>
<p>Praesent venenatis dolor id ante auctor rutrum...</p>
<p>Integer porttitor viverra dignissim... </p>
<p>Aliquam hendrerit accumsan sapien... </p>
</section>
<section>
<h3 id="at">At vero eos et accusamus</a></h3>
<blockquote>At vero eos et accusamus et ...</blockquote>
<p>&#8220;Sed ut perspiciatis unde omnis... &#8221;</p>
</section>
</article>
<footer>
Source: <a href="http://www.lipsum.com/">http://www.lipsum.com/</a>
</footer>
</body>
</html>
```

The structure and parts of a web page which is need to be designed to work on all platforms and be accessible to all users. The markup above the `<body>` tag determines how the document will display, and what is what is within the `<body>` tags determines what the reader will see on the web page.

The details about what each part does and why it is necessary are listed below.

Document Type

This tells what kind of a document it is, HTML5, and what language it uses, English, so a screen reader can correctly pronounce the words.

```
<!DOCTYPE HTML>
<html lang=en>
```

Metadata

This indicates what Unicode character set can be used.

```
<meta charset="utf-8" />
```

Viewport

This allows for the screen to scale depending on which the device it is viewed.

```
<meta name="viewport"content="width=device-width,user-scalable=yes"/>
```

Style Sheet

Cascading style sheets (CSS) give the structured information in the document its shape and are the primary way that how the document looks is separated from what is says.

```
<style type="text/css">
html{margin:0 auto;max-width:33em}
body{font-family:Georgia,serif;padding:.75em 0 .5em .5em}
h1{font-size:115%;font-weight:normal;text-transform:uppercase;
letter-spacing:0.18em}
h2{font-size:115%;font-weight:normal}
h3{font-size:110%;font-weight:normal}
h4{font-size:105%;font-weight:normal}
p{font-size:100%;line-height:1.5em}
a:link{color:#900;text-decoration:none}
a:visited {color:#900;text-decoration:none}
figure {margin:0}
aside{font-size:90%;font-style:italic;margin-left:2em}
</style>
```

CSS3 is essential for the styling, navigation, and general feel of the HTML5 page.

Before you begin the page construction, however, you need to learn about a few of the new HTML5 tags.

Title

It defines the title of the document and will appear above the screen in the navigation bar or tab.

```
<title>Lorem ipsum</title>
```

Header

The example header area contains the page title and subtitle. You use the `<header>` tag to create the content for the header area of the page. The `<header>` tag can contain the opening information about a `<section>` and an `<article>` in addition to the web page itself. The web page created here has a `header` area for the page, which is shown in the high-level design, as well as a header area inside the article and section areas. Here is a `<header>` tag markup example.

```
<header>
<hgroup>
<h1>Title</h1>
<h2>Author</h2>
</hgroup>
<h4><nav><a href="#lorem">Lorem</a> &#183;<a href="#sed"> Praesent
venenatis </a>&#183; <a href="#at">At vero</a></nav></h4>
</header>
```

The `<header>` tag can also contain an `<hgroup>` tag. The `<hgroup>` tag groups headings together, using the `<h1>` to `<h6>` heading levels shown here with a main heading and a sub-heading.

```
<hgroup>
<h1>Title</h1>
<h2>Author</h2>
</hgroup>
```

Navigation

You create the Navigation area of the page using the `<nav>` tag. The `<nav>` element defines an area specifically intended for navigation. The `<nav>` tag should be used for the main site navigation, not to hold links contained in other areas of the page. The navigation area can contain code like that shown below.

```
<h4><nav><a href="#lorem">Lorem</a> &#183;<a href="#sed"> Praesent
venenatis </a> &#183; <a href="#at">At vero</a></nav></h4>
```

Article and Section

The page you are designing contains one Article section, which holds the actual content of the page. You use the `<article>` tag to create this area, and the tag defines content that can be used independently of the other content found on the page. The `<article>` tag marks content that can be removed and placed in another context and be completely understandable.

The Article area in a basic document contains three Section areas. You create these areas using the `<section>` tag. A `<section>` contains the related component areas of web content. The `<section>` tag – and the `<article>` tag, as well – can contain headers, footers, or any other components required to complete the section. The `<section>` tag is for grouping content. The content for both the `<section>` tag and the `<article>` tag usually begins with a `<header>` and ends with a `<footer>`, with the content for the tag in between.

The <section> tag can also contain <article> tags, just as the <article> tag can contain the <section> tag. The <section> tag should be used to group similar information, and the <article> tag should be used for information such as an article or a blog that can be removed and placed in a new context without affecting the meaning of the content. The <article> tag, as its name implies, provides a complete packet of information. In contrast, the <section> tag contains related information, but the information cannot be placed in a different context by itself, because its meaning would be lost.

```
article>
<section>Content</section>
<section>Content</section>
</article>
<section>
<article>Content</article>
<article>Content</article>
</section>
```

Image Elements

Both the <section> and the <article> tags as well as the <header> and <footer> tags can contain the <figure> tag. You use this tag to include images, diagrams, and photos.

The <figure> tag can contain the <figcaption>, which in turn contains the caption for the figure contained in the <figure> tag, allowing you to enter a description that can tie the figure more closely to the content. Here is an example of the <figure> and <figcaption> tag structure.

```
<figure>
<img src="thistlestimothy.jpg"alt="Thistles and timothy, 2010">
<figcaption>Thistles and timothy, 2010</figcaption>
</figure>
```

Aside

Using the <aside> tag createsd the aside area in the basic document. Think of this tag as holding supplementary content that is not part of the flow of the article it supplements. In magazines, asides are frequently used to highlight a point that was made in the article itself. The <aside> tag contains content that can be removed without affecting the information conveyed by the article, section, or page that contains it.

An example of the `<aside>` tag's usage is in the basic document –This is a common fill text. It is in Latin and comes from Cicero.

```
<aside>
<p>This is a common fill text. It is in Latin and comes from
Cicero.</p>
</aside>
```

Footer

The `<footer>` element contains information about a page, article, or section, such as the author or date of the article. It may also show the source for content included in the site.

```
<footer>
Source: <a href="http://www.lipsum.com/"> http://www.lipsum.com/</a>
</footer>
```

Cascading Style Sheets

Cascading style sheets give the structured information in the document its shape – how it looks and is formatted. They are very useful since they separate the form of the document from its content.

They are placed in the `<head>` of the document within `<style>` tags.

```
<style type="text/css">
html{margin:0 auto;max-width:33em}
body{font-family:Georgia,serif;padding:.75em 0 .5em .5em}
h1{font-size:115%;font-weight:normal;text-transform:uppercase;
letter-spacing:0.18em}
h2{font-size:115%;font-weight:normal}
h3{font-size:110%;font-weight:normal}
h4{font-size:105%;font-weight:normal}
p{font-size:100%;line-height:1.5em}
a:link{color:#900;text-decoration:none}
a:visited {color:#900;text-decoration:none}
img{width:20%;height:auto;display:block}
.shapes{width:200%;height:auto;display:block}
</style>
```

The tags above are the ones seen most often. They are included in most websites

The structure of a css entry starts with the elements (see HTML Elements Table), and then within curly brackets {} the properties (see HTML Properties Table) are being specified for the element, such aslike: margin, color, and font-size.

Here are screen shots of the same content with two different style sheets; the first uses the font Georgia and the second, the font Verdana.

DE FINIBUS BONORUM ET MALORUM

Cicero

Lorem ipsum dolor sit amet, consectetuer adipiscing elit, sed diam nonummy nibh euismod tincidunt ut laoreet dolore magna aliquam erat volutpat. Ut wisi enim ad minim veniam, quis nostrud exercitation ulliam corper suscipit lobortis nisl ut aliquip ex ea commodo consequat. Duis autem veleum iriure dolor in hendrerit in vulputate velit esse molestie consequat, vel willum lunombro dolore eu feugiat nulla facilisis at vero eros et accumsan et iusto odio dignissim qui blandit praesent luptatum zzril delenit augue duis dolore te feugait nulla facilisi.

Sed ut perspiciatis unde omnis iste natus error sit voluptatem accusantium doloremque laudantium, totam rem aperiam, eaque ipsa quae ab illo inventore veritatis et quasi architecto beatae vitae dicta sunt explicabo. Nemo enim ipsam voluptatem quia voluptas sit aspernatur aut odit aut fugit, sed quia consequuntur magni dolores eos qui ratione voluptatem sequi nesciunt. Neque porro quisquam est, qui dolorem ipsum quia dolor sit amet, consectetur, adipisci velit, sed quia non numquam eius modi tempora incidunt ut labore et dolore magnam aliquam quaerat voluptatem. Ut enim ad minima veniam, quis nostrum exercitationem ullam corporis suscipit laboriosam, nisi ut aliquid ex ea commodi consequatur? Quis autem vel eum iure reprehenderit qui in ea voluptate velit esse quam nihil molestiae consequatur, vel illum qui dolorem eum fugiat quo voluptas nulla pariatur?

DE FINIBUS BONORUM ET MALORUM

Cicero

Lorem ipsum dolor sit amet, consectetuer adipiscing elit, sed diam nonummy nibh euismod tincidunt ut laoreet dolore magna aliquam erat volutpat. Ut wisi enim ad minim veniam, quis nostrud exercitation ulliam corper suscipit lobortis nisl ut aliquip ex ea commodo consequat. Duis autem veleum iriure dolor in hendrerit in vulputate velit esse molestie consequat, vel willum lunombro dolore eu feugiat nulla facilisis at vero eros et accumsan et iusto odio dignissim qui blandit praesent luptatum zzril delenit augue duis dolore te feugait nulla facilisi.

Sed ut perspiciatis unde omnis iste natus error sit voluptatem accusantium doloremque laudantium, totam rem aperiam, eaque ipsa quae ab illo inventore veritatis et quasi architecto beatae vitae dicta sunt explicabo. Nemo enim ipsam voluptatem quia voluptas sit aspernatur aut odit aut fugit, sed quia consequuntur magni dolores eos qui ratione voluptatem sequi nesciunt. Neque porro quisquam est, qui dolorem ipsum quia dolor sit amet, consectetur, adipisci velit, sed quia non numquam eius modi tempora incidunt ut labore et dolore magnam aliquam quaerat voluptatem. Ut enim ad minima veniam, quis nostrum exercitationem ullam corporis suscipit laboriosam, nisi ut aliquid ex ea commodi consequatur? Quis autem vel eum iure reprehenderit qui in ea voluptate velit esse quam nihil molestiae consequatur, vel illum qui dolorem eum fugiat quo voluptas nulla pariatur?

External and Print Style Sheets

The style sheet can also an external file and linked to the html document like this:

```
<link rel="stylesheet" type="text/css" href="foo.css" media="screen">
```

For material that will be printed as well as viewed online, you need to link a print style sheet in the `<head>` of the document. The link looks like this:

```
<link rel="stylesheet"type="text/css"href="print.css"media="print">
```

A print style sheet will usually specify a smaller font size, about 75% of the default size, and does not include a maximum width.

For example: `body{margin:0 auto;font-size:12px;}`

Geometric Shapes Made with CSS3

Using CSS3, it is possible to make a variety of geometric shapes, like this triangle, square, and circle. Details about making them are in the Small Graphics chapter.

Presenting Information

In web design, like most other things we do, context needs to be looked at carefully and in detail. The more we understand about what we want to do, the particulars of what we are trying to say, and in what contexts and what ways it will be received, the more effective we can be.

Although websites come in many different forms, most take one of three general formats, and each of these formats is used differently. Understanding these differences, how they function, and how design principles can fail if misapplied helps in understanding how to best design a particular site. Each asks for its own set of principles and a focus on what problems are being solved.

Much bad web design is based on trying to apply an idea that works for one form to another where it doesn't – for instance, the elimination of white space in a site, which presents extended text.

These are the three:

1. **A story.** – Extended text, as is found in many online newspapers, blog entries, news magazines, and stories. Because these are read like essays, many of the traditional guides for print typography can be applied effectively to stories and other narratives such as font size, line length, line height, and white space. Examples of extended text are an essay, a newspaper story, and a novel, like this beginning of essay by George Orwell.

Politics and the English Language, 1946

George Orwell

Most people who bother with the matter at all would admit that the English language is in a bad way, but it is generally assumed that we cannot by conscious action do anything about it. Our civilization is decadent and our language – so the argument runs – must inevitably share in the general collapse. It follows that any struggle against the abuse of language is a sentimental archaism, like preferring candles to electric light or hansom cabs to aeroplanes. Underneath this lies the half-conscious belief that language is a natural growth and not an instrument which we shape for our own purposes.

Now, it is clear that the decline of a language must ultimately have political and economic causes: it is not due simply to the bad influence of this or that individual writer. But an effect can become a cause, reinforcing the original cause and producing the same effect in an intensified form, and so on indefinitely. A man may take to drink because he feels himself to be a failure, and then fail all the more completely because he drinks. It is rather the same thing that is happening to the English language. It becomes ugly and inaccurate

2. **A collection.** – Information presented as tabular data, such as tables and lists of various kinds. They can be organized a number of ways and combinations of these ways – by alphabet, number, location, kind, time, or sequence and in an order of relationships, a hierarchy. "Density is the new whitespace" is good advice for online collections (as it is in print collections – dictionaries, catalogues, want ads, and phone directories) because they are scanned for a particular bit or bits of information, not read over a period of time. Efficient (and dense) ways of organizing information are at the center of their usefulness.

Four of the ways to present a collection of information are as a table, an ordered list, an unordered list, and a definition list.

TABLE EXAMPLE

Using a Keyboard to Navigate Websites

If you want to –	Select
Forward from link to link or to controls	Tab
Backward from link to link or to controls	Shift + Tab
Select buttons	Spacebar

If you want to –	Select
Navigate and select radio buttons	Arrow
Select/deselect boxes	Spacebar
Move from box to box	Tab
Open a list box	ALT + Down arrow
Read the prior screen	CTRL(⌘) + Page Up
Read the next screen	CTRL(⌘) + Page Down
Go to the top of the page	CTRL(⌘) + Up arrow
Go to the bottom of the page	CTRL(⌘) + Down arrow
Refresh the screen	F5
Go back a page	ALT + Left Arrow
Go forward a page	ALT + Right Arrow
Highlight URL in address bar	CTRL(⌘) + L
Hide a page	CTRL(⌘) + H
Copy selected text	CTRL(⌘) + C
Paste selected text	CTRL(⌘) + V

Other examples are the different tables included in this book, like HTML Elements and Properties.

List Examples

The ingredients list uses an unordered list `<ul>` and the directions an ordered list `<ol>`.

Granola Recipe

Ingredients

- 6 cups rolled oats
- 2 cups walnuts
- 1 cup water
- ½ cup sugar
- 1 cup peanut oil
- 2 cups raisins

Directions

1. Preheat over to 275°F (135°C).
2. Mix oats and walnuts in a large bowl.
3. Dissolve sugar in warm water.
4. Add water and oil to oats and walnuts.
5. Stir and let soak for 10 minutes.
6. Spread in baking pan.
7. Cook in oven for 3 to 3½ hours, until lightly browned.
8. Cool and add raisins.

Here is an example of a definition list `<dl>`:

Bug

insect (bug on a leaf)
germ (caught the bug)
covert listening device (the room was bugged)
defect in software (it has a bug)
Volkswagen Beetle
annoying (bug me)
enthusiast (camera bug)
to go away (bug out)
bulge (bug out, bug eyed)

3. **A visual.**– Single message sites, like headings, trademarks, slides, Signs,or ads. These are like a snapshot, an aphorism, or a doorway – words or images or a function taken in quickly, at a glance.

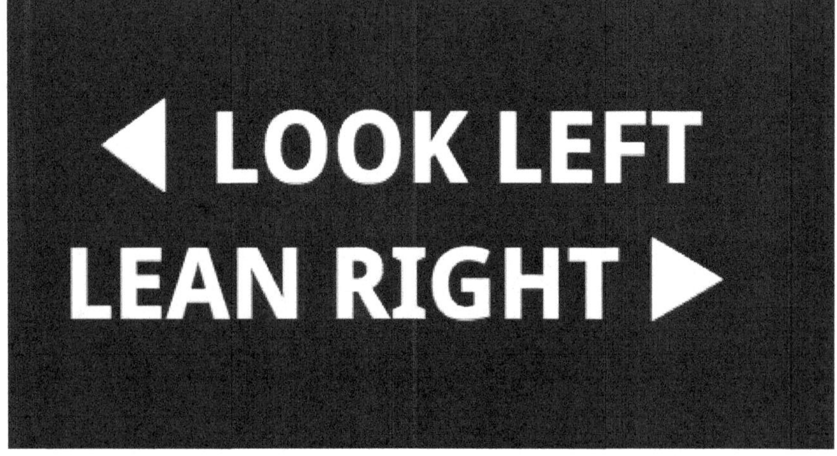

This is the markup for LOOK LEFT LEAN RIGHT:

```
font-size:380%;color:#fff; padding:1em 1em 1em .5em;background-
color:#000;font-weight:700;font-family:'droid sans',sans-
serif;text-align:center; margin:0
```

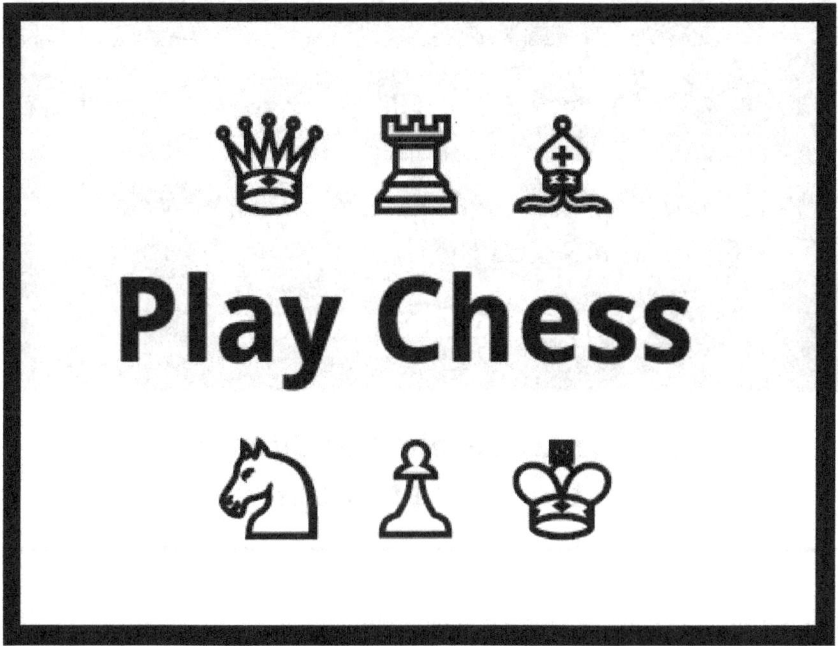

This is the markup for Play Chess: `font-size: 450%; color:#000; padding: .5em;background-color:#fff;font-weight:700;font-family:'droid sans',sans-serif;text-align:center; margin:.25em 0; border-width: .2em; border-style:solid; border-color:#000`

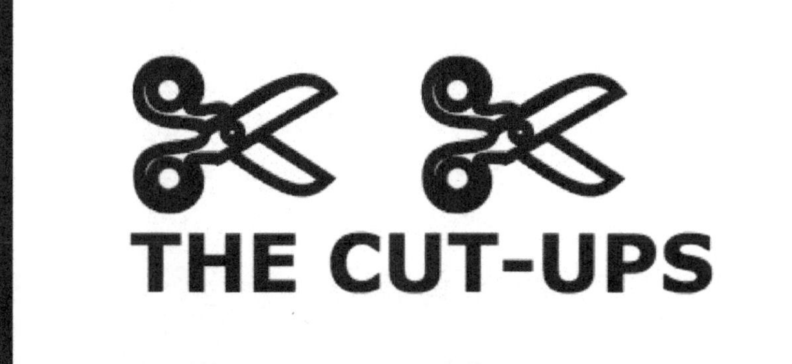

This is the Dingbat used for Cut-Ups: #9988

And a list can also be presented as a graphic:

Sentences are short.

The text is broken down into short paragraphs.

Favour the active voice.

Do not use jargon, slang or idiomatic phrases.

There are links to definitions of technical terms.

Simple and Clear Language

Making Accessible Web Sites for the United Nations

This is from UN Guidelines for accessible websites.

These designs make a point, but visually as an image, not as story told over time or as a grid filled with information.

Availability and Efficiency

Making websites available to as many people as possible is an important goal for any designer, as is making files that download quickly. To do both, be sparing with the size of the files and careful with their structure.

Text is the best way to accomplish this and is also the easiest medium for creating websites, as well as simplest and quickest to edit, proof, correct, and to locate information in.

Photographs, Other Media Than Text

For comparison with files in other formats, the size of the file of a text document in html is about 2 KB for contents of an average page in a book, or 200 KB for 100 pages.

Here are four examples of the same photograph saved a 24-bit and an 8-bit png file and as a maximum quality and a low quality jpg files.

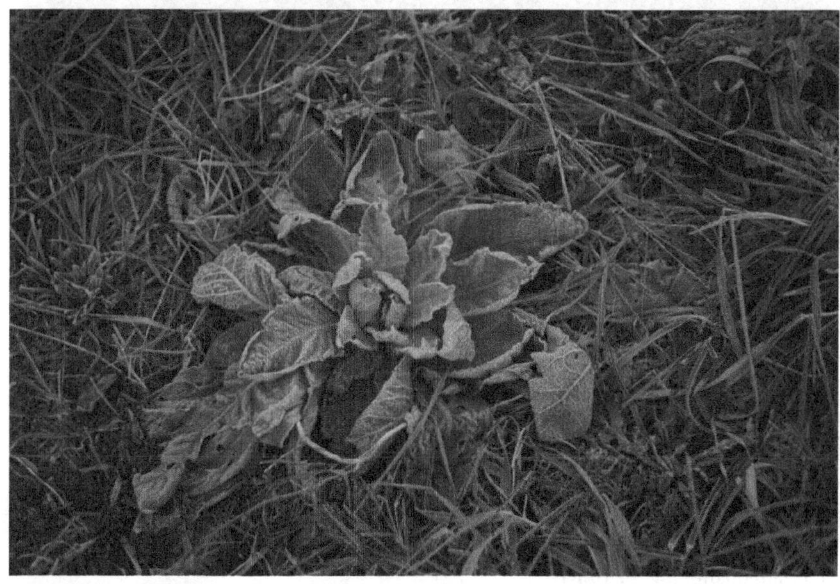

24bit png – 358KB

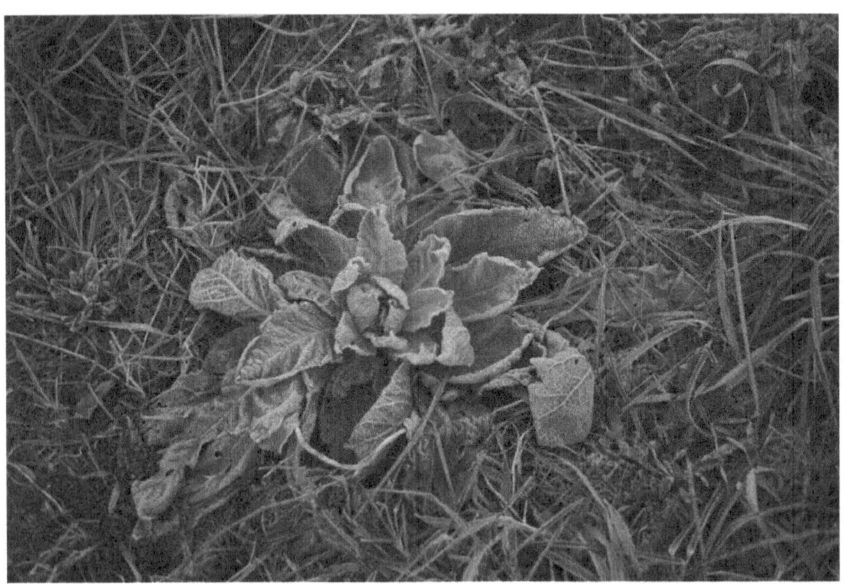

8-bit png – 122 KB

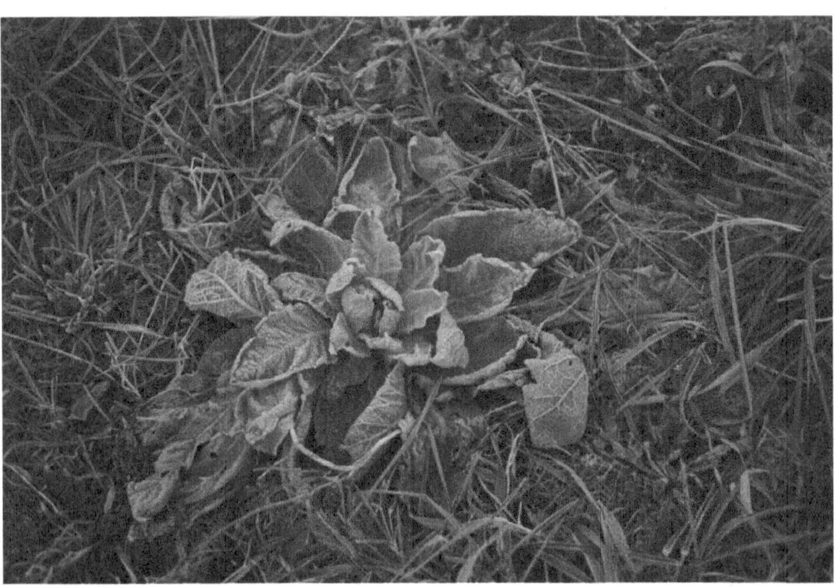

Maximum quality jpg – 248 KB

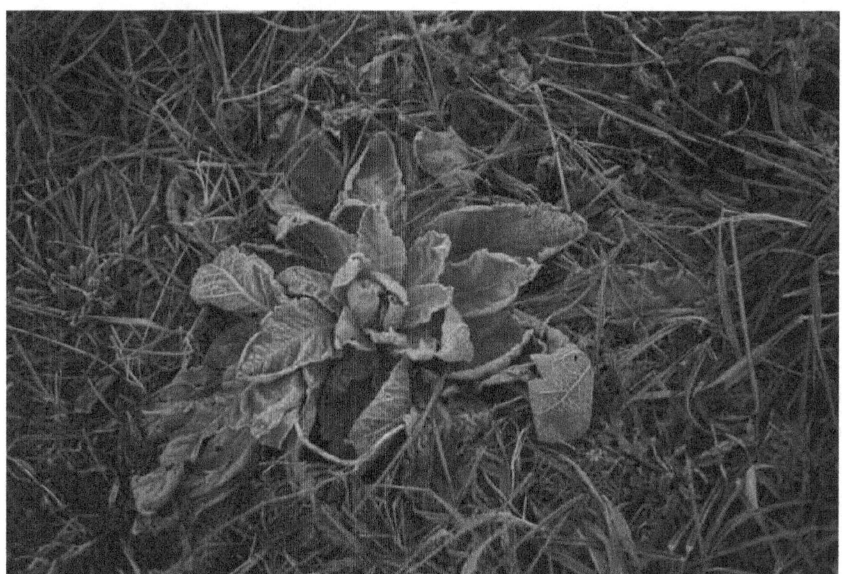

Low-quality jpg – 38 KB

If you are placing photographic images in your sites, it is important to consider the size of the files and whether the lower resolution means a loss of meaning and the feelings you want to get across.

And when you put something other than text in html up on a website – pdfs, videos, audio files, animations, photographs, graphics, make sure:

They add something text cannot; otherwise, it is a waste of peoples' time and bandwidth.

That content in them is accessible to those who can't see or hear it and that it will work on different devices.

That you are willing to have your site available only to those with a broadband connection, especially if what you have added is a video. (In 2013, less than 15% of the world's population has broadband [4 MB downstream], as compared with about one-half who have an Internet connection.)

Video and Media Other Than Text

Some other things to be sure to consider when using videos, animations, or information graphics based on images for teaching in place of text, with or without illustrations, are:

How much more time does it take to watch and hear the information in a video or animation than to read it?

Is the information graphic easy to follow and is it accessible?

How easy is it to go back and review the material presented?
How easy is it to search for a word, a sentence, a name, a chart, or a diagram that was shown?
How difficult is it to edit, update, or correct other media compared to a text document?
How many specialized skills do the different media require to produce and edit them? Are they available? How much will they add to the cost?

Application Cache

Using the application cache so that the files will be available to the user when they are offline is especially important as more and more people are using phones to access information on the Internet, and they are frequently without a connection, or it is too expensive to use for long periods of time that reading a long text requires.

It involves include markup similar to this in the head of your page:

```
<html manifest="example.appcache">
```

and making a cache manifest file and saving it to site directory; for example:

```
<CACHE MANIFEST>
index.html
introduction.html
frostmullein.jpg
rectpercent.svg
```

Although most browsers do cache files, using a cache manifest means there is enough space – 4M – given to it to store four or five book-length html files.

Text & Typography

Basics

Most of web design is the designing of text – picking the fonts to use and shaping them with style sheets. The primary goal in designing text is to make it transparent, so it can be looked through, not looked at. The fonts are there to support the information it presents, without intruding on it.

Legibility is the degree to which glyphs (individual characters) in text are understandable or recognizable based on appearance. "The legibility of a typeface is related to the characteristics inherent in its design . . . which relate to the ability to distinguish one letter from the other." Legibility includes factors such as "x-height, character shapes, stroke contrast, the size of its counters, serifs or lack thereof, and weight."

Legibility is different from readability, which refers to entire words, sentences, and paragraphs. Readability is influenced by line length, primary and secondary leading, justification, typestyle, kerning, tracking, and point size, etc.

Readability is the ease in which text can be read and understood.

In practical application some attributes cross over and affect both readability and legibility.

How paragraphs are presented is a central part of the design of useful and unobtrusive text. Following these directions can make them easier to read.

For paragraphs – the `<p>` tag – use:

Line height between 1.3 and 1.6 em.

Font-size on the web of between 16 px and 18 px, depending on x-height of the font. For instance, here are two, Cambria with tall x-height and Garamond with short one:

> Cambria: The sound is forc'd, the notes are few!
> Garamond: The sound is forc'd, the notes are few!

A text width between 30 and 35 em; – this page is set at 33 em.

A small reduction in word' spacing can make the text flow more evenly: `word-spacing: -0.05em`

And don't justify the text. It makes large word spaces and those disrupt reading.

In all the text, including paragraphs, use:

Smart quotes ‘ ’ ‘ ’ “ ” “ ” – not generic quotes ' " "

A smart apostrophe’ ʼ – not a generic one ' '

An – (en dash – or –) with a space on either side, instead of – (em dash —) with no spaces.

Use Unicode for special characters – é not é for é, and“ not ” for “.

In the tables you will find a table is one of HTML Entities, a list of some of the commonly used entities, – those used for punctuation, accented letters, and common symbols.

Emphasis within a paragraph *should* be done using the <em> tag, not underlined – <u> tag, nor **bold** – <strong> or <b> tag, nor ALL CAPS. The latter three distract from ease of reading a long text because they disrupt its flow.

Bold and all caps, both **TOGETHER and** SEPARATELY, are usually used only for titles and headings.

Any Unicode character can be inserted into a web page using either decimal or hexadecimal format in two different ways: The decimal can be in the short form (A A) or the long form (A A), as can the hexadecimal – short form (A A) or long form (A A)

Many common fractions can be presented in two ways; – for instance: 1/4 or ¼, 3/8 or ⅜. **This table** shows the latter ones, which are included in Unicode.

Fonts

If someone says san-serif fonts are better than serif fonts, or the reverse, always ask which fonts they mean, since Georgia 123 ≠ Times New Roman 123 and Verdana 123 ≠ Arial 123.

Also ask what font-size, line-height, and line-length will be used; – those often matter more for readability than the font chosen.

Here are six commonly used fonts, three serif – Georgia, Times New Roman, Palatino, and three sans serif – Arial, Verdana, Lucida Grande. Arial requires some letter spacing so the r doesn't run into the n and make an m. The font size for these is 16px, so their individual characteristic can be more clearly seen. At the end of each font entry isare: 1lI rm jg to so that those characters which sometimes cause problems with legibility can be seen.

These are the fonts set at larger size so the differences are clear.

This serif font is Georgia and set at font-size 1.5 em, word-spacing: -0.01em. 1lI rn jg

This serif font is Times New Roman and set at font size 1.5 em, word-spacing: -0.025em. 1lI rn jg

This serif font is Palatino and set at font-size 1.5 em, word-spacing: -0.01em. 1lI rn jg

This sans-serif font is Arial and set at font-size 1.5 em, word-spacing: -0.095em, letter-spacing: 0.01em. 1lI rn jg

This sans-serif font is Verdana and set at font-size 1.5 em, word-spacing: -0.095em. 1lI rn jg

This sans-serif font is Lucida Grande and set at font-size 1.5 em, word-spacing: -0.05em. 1lI rn jg

Legibility and Readability

Legibility and readability are terms that are often used when typography is discussed, and they do at times overlap in meaning. These are some of the differences between the two terms and how they are used.

Legibility

Legible comes from the Latin *legere*, meaning able to be read or deciphered. Legibility refers to how easily one letter can be distinguished from another. Legibility is the degree to which letters in the text are understandable or recognizable based on appearance. "The legibility of a typeface is related to the characteristics inherent in its design . . . which relate to the ability to distinguish one letter from the other." Legibility includes factors such as "x-height, character shapes, stroke contrast, the size of its counters, serifs or lack thereof, and weight."

Factors such as x-height, counter size, letter spacing, and stroke width are more significant for legibility than the presence or absence of serifs.

Design Features That Make a Typeface Legible

Large X-Height

A large x-height increases the negative space within each letter. This makes its shape much more discernible.

Large Counters

The negative space within a letter is called a counter. When a typeface has large counters, it is easier to distinguish the shape of each individual letter.

Simple Letterforms

The simpler a letterform, the more legible it is. Sans-serif types are generally more legible than their serif counterparts because they do not have any serifs interfering with the shapes of the letters. However, this does not mean that sans serifs are necessarily easier to *read* in text. Actually, serif types are generally considered *more* readable.

Readability

Use Contrast.

Text is easier to read when the font color and the background color have a strong contrast – usually black (`hex #000`) on white (`hex #fff`), the widest separation of light and dark.

Use Short Paragraphs.

They are easier to grasp, follow, and locate information in. Information in long paragraphs is often difficult to follow and remember. It is also easier to find details the reader wants to return to.

Use Headings and Lists.

They help the readers understand the main points and put them in order. They also make it easy for the readers to locate again an idea or sequence of ideas that interests them.

Create Emphasis.

Within the body of a sentence use italics for *emphasis*, not **bold text**. The use of bold within the body of the text disrupts ease of reading. Bold should be used for titles and headings.

Do Not Set your Font Size in Pixels.

Leave it as the default, which is 16 px in most browsers, and set the size for different elements with relative measures – % and em. The setting for paragraphs <p> should be between 100% and 110%, or 1 em and 1.1 em, depending on the font used.

Consider Serif and Sans-Serif Fonts.

It is not possible to make a meaningful judgment about readability between serif and sans-serif fonts in general. They vary so much from one font to another. For instance, compare these commonly used fonts: Georgia jgh 1lI to Times New Roman jgh 1lI and Verdana jgh 1lI to Arial jgh 1lI. They have to be compared one to one and a judgment reached on that comparison.

Consider Text Width, Line Height.

For text width, which set in your style sheet, paragraphs should be between 30 and 35 em (60 to 70 letters and spaces). The line height – the space between the lines – works best at between 1.3 and 1.5 em (an em is the width of the lower case m in the font you have chosen).

Use Color for Your Links.

Red is the traditional color for calling attention to text within a document. Links can be both within the text or listed separately, depending on how they are being used. It is especially important that all technical terms be linked to a definition.

Presentations & Projection

Nearly all presentations are, in one way or another, difficult to understand and follow, not because of the speakers, but because of problems with the projected slides.

Some of the Problems

The room is rarely completely dark, so colors and values are diluted by the light in the room, either from overhead lights or through the blinds. The latter is especially bad on a sunny day.

Projectors enlarge the image greatly, so you cannot count on very much detail in the text or images. Most visual subtleties are lost.

Many presentations are developed on a computer screen that is backlit and has a high resolution and good dynamic range–all of which are missing when the slides are projected.

The audience usually sees the screen from very different viewpoints. The rooms are not like a movie theater, narrow and deep, but like a classroom, broad and shallow.

The presenters only have the vaguest idea of what can be seen by the audience because they are often facing them and looking back over their shoulder to see the screen.

How can these problems be addressed?

If possible, all presentations should be previewed in the place where they will be given.

Don't try to put more information up than can be easily read as projected on the screen and give the audience time enough to read it.

Work with black on white text and be careful with font size, line length, and word spacing. This can minimize the loss in readability due to light dilution of the slides.

If you use Arial, be sure to use a small amount of letter spacing (.01 em) so the r and n don't run together and make an m (then yarn won't look like yam).

Don't use fonts with hairline serifs (common ones are **Bodoni**, **Didot**, and **Walbaum**) because the thin serifs disappear when projected.

If photographic images are used, try taking them into Photoshop and increasing the contrast and saturation to make them visually more effective when projected.

Make your presentation in html and post it to the web. Then it will be easy to scale on the screen and available to anyone who wants to review it later.

Presentations are difficult because there are so many variables that are not in your control–the quality of the projector, the surface it is projected on, the light in the room, and the different relationships of the audience to the screen.

Because of those problems, it is best to stick to text or line graphics in black and white. Be sure your presentation can be made large enough to be read, darken the room as much as possible, and don›t expect anything but the coarsest information to be communicated by color.

Avoid any presentation software. Use html. It is easy to prepare, edit, and revise, if necessary, on the spot.

The Bill of Rights as a Model

Original Ten Amendments: The Bill of Rights

Passed by Congress September 25, 1789.
Ratified December 15, 1791.

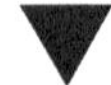

Screen Shot of First Slide

Because they are html files, if formatted well, they can be viewed on phones, tablets of all sizes, desktop computers, and flat panel displays, as well as projected.

In addition, html files allow the author, using a print style sheet, to format the slides for printing in an easy to read and use format, as in the illustration below.

Original Ten Amendments: The Bill of Rights

Passed by Congress September 25, 1789.
Ratified December 15, 1791.

Amendment I
Freedoms, Petitions, Assembly

Congress shall make no law respecting an establishment of religion, or prohibiting the free exercise thereof; or abridging the freedom of speech, or of the press, or the right of the people peaceably to assemble, and to petition the Government for a redress of grievances.

Amendment II
Right to bear arms

A well regulated Militia, being necessary to the security of a free State, the right of the people to keep and bear Arms, shall not be infringed.

Amendment III
Quartering of soldiers

No Soldier shall, in time of peace be quartered in any house, without the consent of the Owner, nor in time of war, but in a manner to be prescribed by law.

Amendment IV
Search and arrest

The right of the people to be secure in their persons, houses, papers, and effects, against unreasonable searches and seizures, shall not be violated, and no Warrants shall issue, but upon probable cause, supported by Oath or affirmation, and particularly describing the place to be searched, and the persons or things to be seized.

Amendment V
Rights in criminal cases

No person shall be held to answer for a capital, or otherwise infamous crime, unless on a presentment or indictment of a Grand Jury, except in cases arising in the land or naval forces, or in the Militia, when in actual service in time of War or public danger; nor shall any person be subject for the same offence to be twice put in jeopardy of life or limb, nor shall be compelled in any criminal case to be a witness against himself, nor be deprived of life, liberty, or property, without due process of law; nor shall private property be taken for public use, without just compensation.

Amendment VI
Right to a fair trial

In all criminal prosecutions, the accused shall enjoy the right to a speedy and public trial, by an impartial jury of the State and district wherein the crime shall have been committed;

Screen Shot of First Print Page

The main differences between the two style sheets are font size and weight and padding in the `<nav>` tag.

In the screen style sheet the `<nav>` is set like this:

```
nav{font-size:100%;font-weight:900;padding:2em 0 60em 0}
```

And in the print style sheet the font size set at 12 px and normal weight and the `<nav>` is set like this:

```
nav{padding:0;margin:0}
```

This site is also accessible to the blind and can be navigated with keystrokes, as well as a mouse or touch, depending on the device used.

Working in this way with html, it is possible to make the slide presentation available to everyone in whatever format, in file that is only 5.8 K, so it makes minimal demands on the network and local storage.

It is also small in size and accessible and an easy model to follow. Here is a shortened version of the code:

```
<!DOCTYPE HTML>
<html>
<head>
<meta charset="utf-8" />
<meta name="viewport"content="width=device-width,user-scalable=yes"/>
<link href='http://fonts.googleapis.com/css?family=Droid+Sans:400,
700' rel='stylesheet' type='text/css'>
<style type="text/css">
html{margin:0 auto;max-width:33em}
body{font-family:'droid sans',sans-serif;font-size:17px;margin:0
1em 0 1em}
h1{font-size:140%;font-weight:700;padding:1em 0 0 0}
h2{font-size:125%;font-weight:700; line-height:1.3em; padding:
1.5em 0 0 0 }
h3{font-size:115%;font-weight:bold}
h4{font-size:110%;font-weight:bold;padding:2em 0 60em 0}
p{font-size:100%;font-weight:700; line-height:1.5em;}
.dot{color:#fff}
.arrow{font-size:125%;font-weight:700;color:#ddd;text-align:left}
a.arrow:link { color: #ddd; }
```

```
a.arrow:visited { color: #ddd; }
a.arrow:hover { color: #666; }
.top{padding:4em 0 0 0}
</style>
<link rel="stylesheet" type="text/css" href="slideprint.css"
media="print">
<title>Original Ten Amendments</title>
</head>
<body>
<article>
<h1 id="one">Original Ten Amendments:<br> The Bill of Rights</h1>
<p>Passed by Congress September 25, 1789.<br>
Ratified December 15, 1791.
<h4>
<nav> <a class="arrow" href="#two">▼</a></nav></h4>
<section>
<h2 id="two">Amendment I</h2>
<h3>Freedoms, Petitions, Assembly</h3>
<p>Congress shall make no law respecting an establishment of reli-
gion, or prohibiting the free exercise thereof; or abridging the
freedom of speech, or of the press, or the right of the people
peaceably to assemble, and to petition the Government for a redress
of grievances.
</a><h4>
...
</body>
</html>
```

Here is the print style sheet:

```
@charset "UTF-8";
body{margin:0 auto;font-size: 12px;} h1{padding:1em 0 0 0}
h2{padding:0;margin:0} h3{padding:0;margin:0}
h4{font-size:110%;font-weight:bold;padding:0;margin:0}
.dot{margin:0; padding:0}
.arrow{font-size:10%;font-weight:700;color:#fff;
text-align:left} p{font-weight:400; margin:0;padding:0}
section{padding:0;padding:0}
```

Here is a second example that includes an image as well as text and navigation with text so it is easy to go back and forth in the presentation.

Cheesy Picante Quesadillas

All you need is 20 minutes and four ingredients to make these tasty quesadillas, oozing with melted cheese and flavored with picante sauce and green chiles.

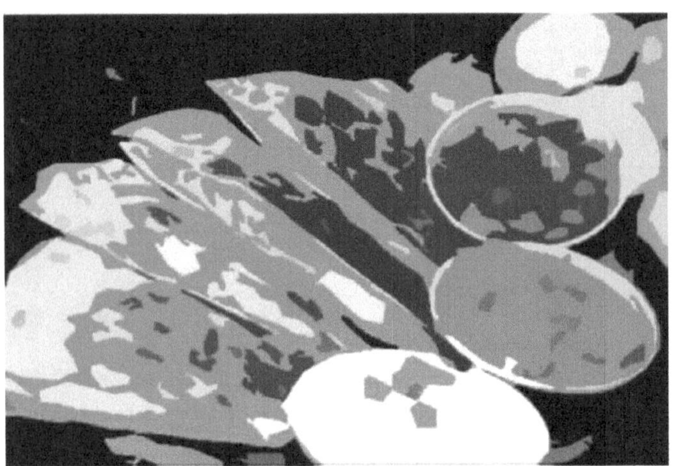

Top · Ingredients · Directions · Time

Here is part of the code showing the navigation to the four parts of the presentation:

```
<hgroup> <h1 class="dot" id="top"> &#183;</a></h1><h1>Cheesy
Picante Quesadillas</h1>
<p>All you need is 20 minutes and four ingredients to make these
tasty quesadillas, oozing with melted cheese and flavored with
picante sauce and green chiles.</p>
<img src="quesadillacutout.jpg" alt="Quesadillas">
</hgroup>
<h4><nav> <a href="#top">Top</a> &#183; <a href="#ingredients">Ingr
edients</a></a> &#183; <a href="#directions">Directions</a> &#183;
<a href="#time">Time</a></nav></h4>
```

Writing

Writing for the Web requires thoughtfulness, attention to detail, and modesty.

The Web is a personal and intimate medium, and writing is your primary means of communication on it.

It is like a conversation, so keep that tone of voice. You seldom need to shout or whisper.

With these things in mind, here are some suggestions for doing it well:

Try keeping your sentences short, so they are easy to read and understand quickly. Make sure you don't include any unnecessary words. Simple sentences are easier to grasp quickly than complex ones.

When you have a choice, use familiar words and ones that are easy to picture. Don't use long words, especially technical terms, if you can avoid them. Define technical terms if you do use them.

You will lose your reader if you include errors in spelling and grammar, as well as in fact. Be sure to check all of them before you post your work.

Showing off, along with being cute and vain, are other ways to lose your reader. Remember that you want to speak to others and provide them with useful information, not sell yourself. Your writing is should be one side of a conversation, not a speech to a crowd.

Use italics for emphasis in your paragraphs, not all-caps or bold text, so it doesn't interrupt or distract the reader.

Use headings to divide the text into clear sections, so it is easy to scan to find particular subjects and details.

Use exclamation marks and emoticons rarely, if at all.

Information Graphics

Information graphics are a common way to present information on the Web. Some are difficult to follow due to confusing designs and lack of contrasts. They are also often inaccessible to the disabled because they are not built on text. Here are some examples, which are easy to read and follow and accessible to all.

The first is a list.

Food

1 – Buy it with thought.
2 – Cook it with care.
3 – Serve just enough.
4 – Save what will keep.
5 – Eat what would spoil.
6 – Home-grown is best.

Don't waste it.

The second is the same information presented in a table and in a bar chart, using SVG.

Ratio of Pay - CEO:Avg Worker

Country	Ratio of Pay - CEO to Avg Worker
Japan	11 to 1
Germany	12 to 1
France	15 to 1
Italy	20 to 1
Canada	20 to 1
South Africa	21 to 1
Britain	22 to 1
Mexico	47 to 1
Venezula	50 to 1
United States	475 to 1

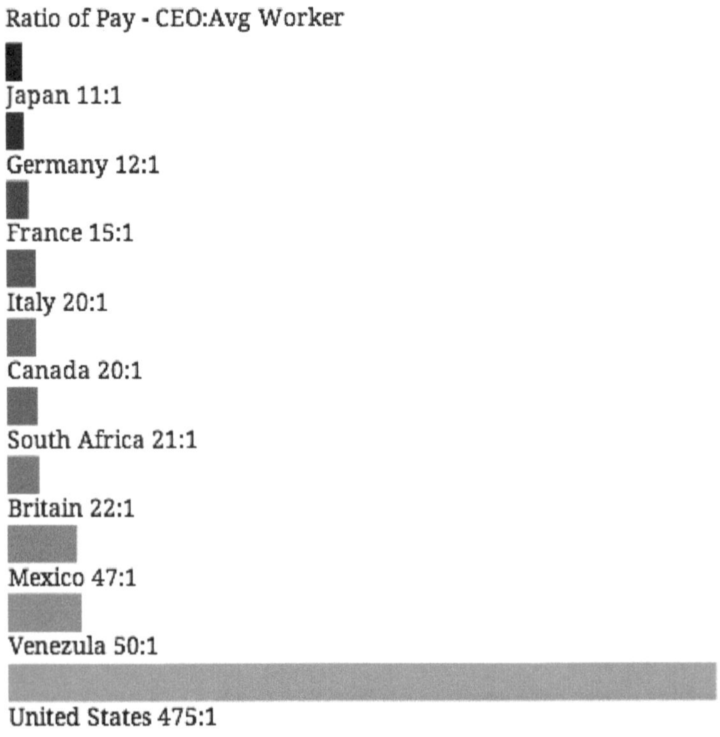

Ratio of Pay - CEO:Avg Worker

Japan 11:1

Germany 12:1

France 15:1

Italy 20:1

Canada 20:1

South Africa 21:1

Britain 22:1

Mexico 47:1

Venezula 50:1

United States 475:1

The third is two bar charts presenting the same information with different layouts, but using the same css for the bars.

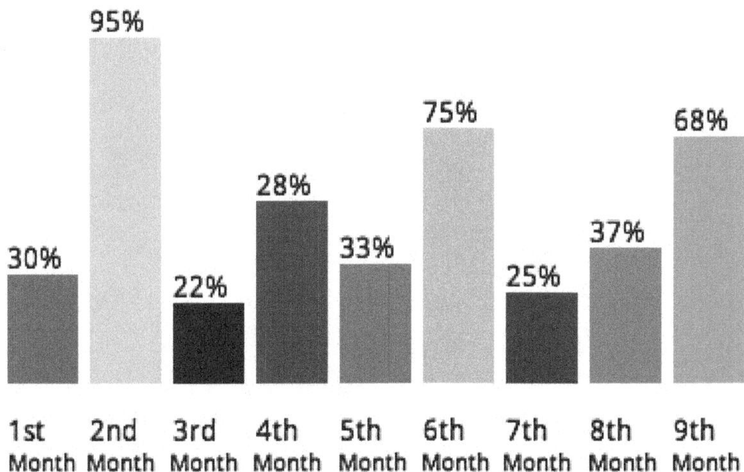

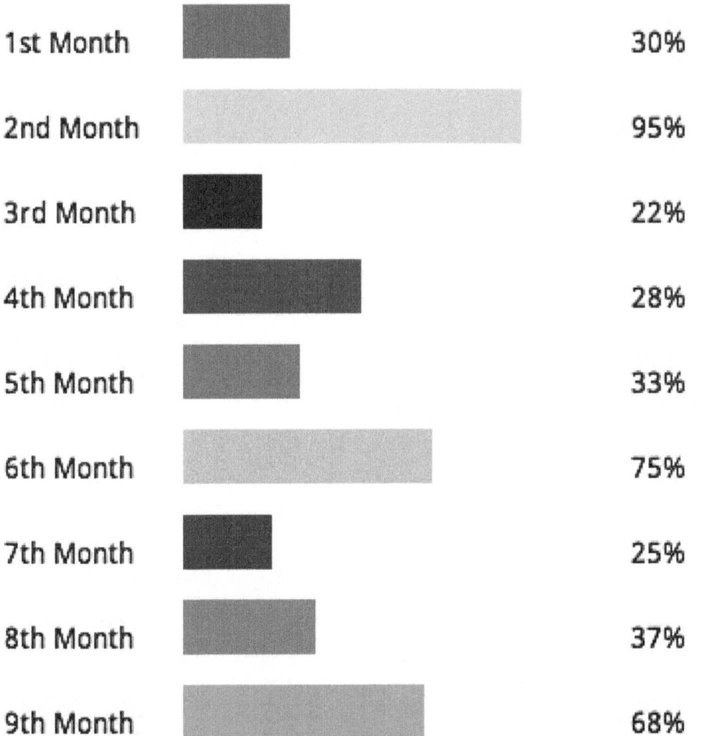

Small Graphics using Unicode, CSS, and SVG

Web pages are becoming large and larger, recently reaching an average of more than 1 Mb for one page. Much of the increase has come from different kinds of image and sound files, which are many times larger than a file based on text.

There are several different ways to include graphics in web pages thatw take up very little space, usually about one-tenth as much, as a bitmap file. Bitmap files also scale to different sizes and download quickly, both helpful to those who have a slow connection or who want to project their files.

Three of the formats that can give small, efficient graphics are those that come with Unicode, those that are included in CSS3, and those that can be made using Scalable Vector Graphics (SVG).

Unicode

Unicode is a computing industry standard for encoding, representing, ation and handling of text expressed in most of the world's writing systems. It has 110,182 graphical, formatting, and control characters, covering the different letters, characters, and sounds, as well as, many mathematical, musical, and other symbols.

Tables of the four different groups of Unicode are included in the Tables and Lists section.

Here are four of the sets of symbols and graphical elements that are included in Unicode.

Dingbats

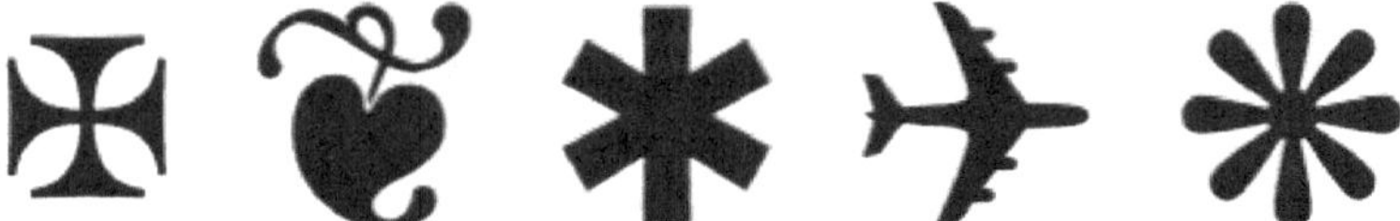

A border made using the characters `#10096` and `#10097`.

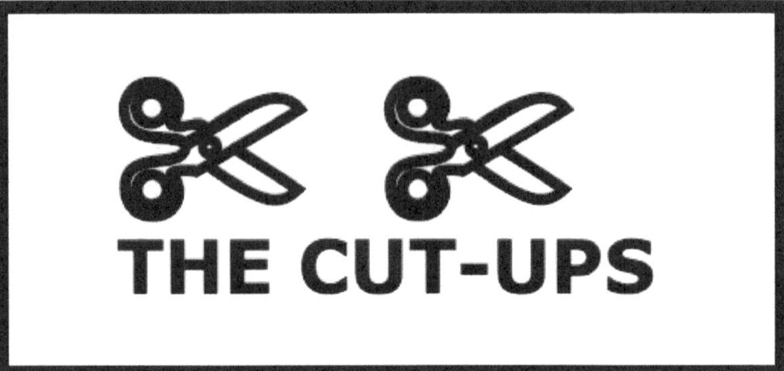

A title for a brand.

Miscellaneous Symbols

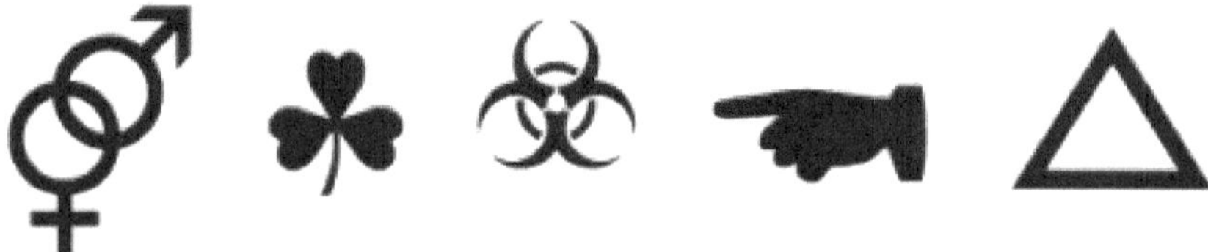

A border made using the characters `#9901` and `#9899`.

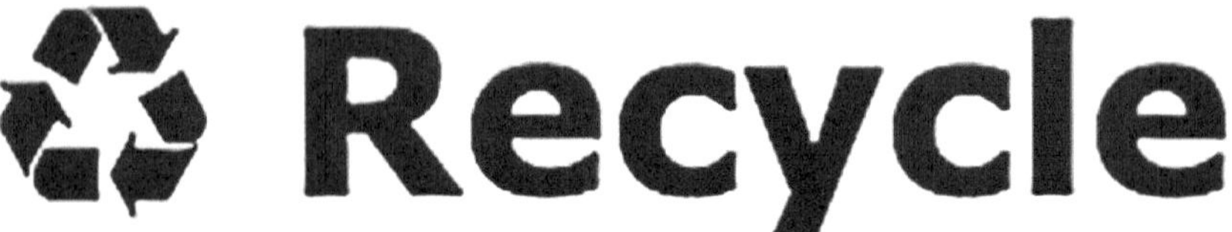

For social action.

Geometric Shapes

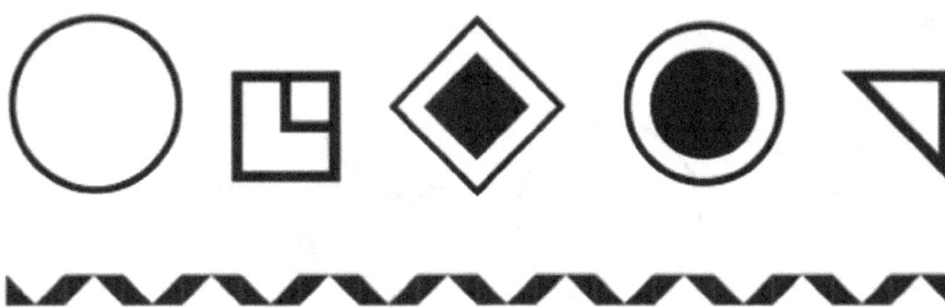

A border made using the characters #9699, #9698, #9700, and #9701.

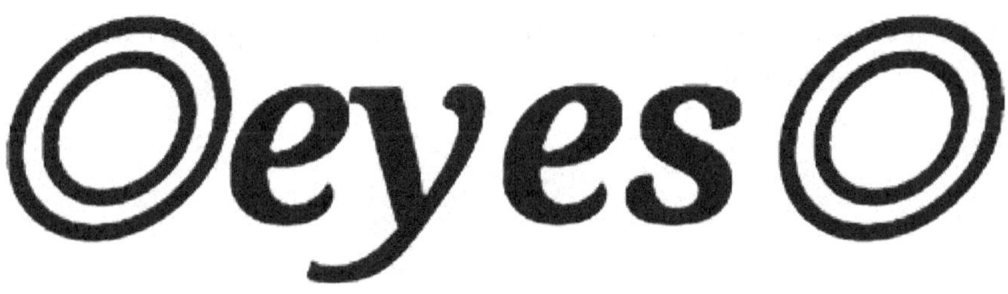

A business logo

Block Elements

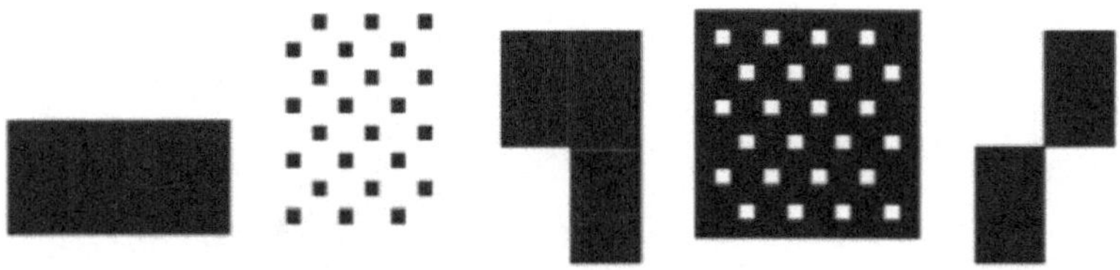

A border made using the characters #9627, #9628, #9629, and #9630.

aroundtheblock

A neighborhood logo.

CSS: Circle, Star, and Triangle

A list of some simple CSS shapes and how to mark them up is included in the Tables and Lists section.

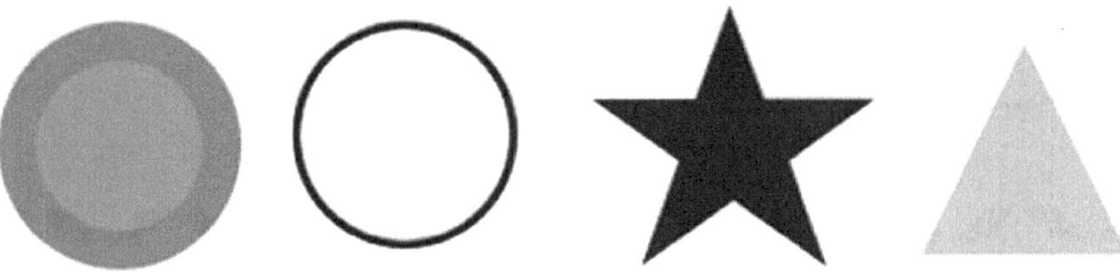

SVG : Scalable Vector Graphics

A list of a few common SVG shapes and how to mark them up is included in the Tables and Lists section.

Circle, square, and triangle.

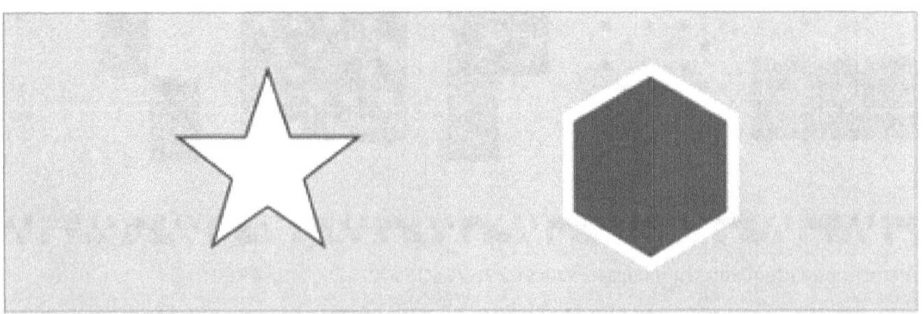

Rectangle, star, and polygon

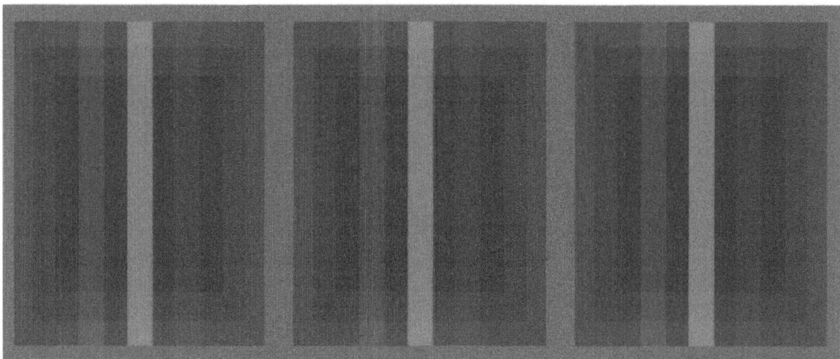

Rectangles and transparency.

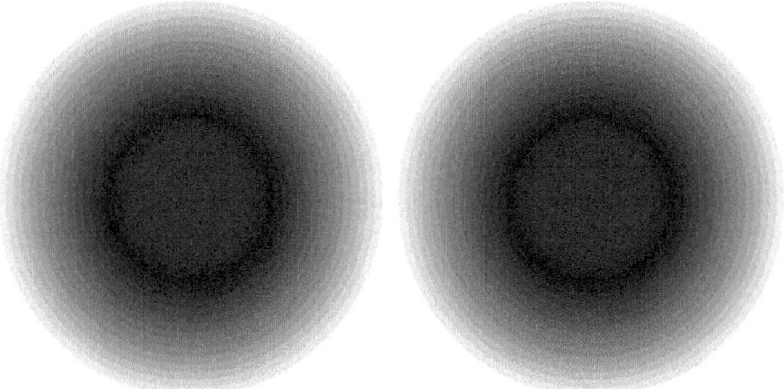

An example of a very small SVG file (1.4 K), repeated twice.

Three Checklists

For Validity, Accessibility, and Ease of Use

1. Validate the file. HTML Validation:- `validator.w3.org`; CSS Validation:- `jigsaw.w3.org/css-validator`
2. Test it for accessibility, giving special attention to gray scale contrast. WAVE:- `wave.webaim.org`
3. Test for speed. PageSpeed:- `developers.google.com/speed/pagespeed`
4. Test for usability by the colorblind. Colorblind Web Page Filter: `colorfilter.wickline.org`
5. Try it in Safari Speech on a Mac, or use another screen reader on another operating system to double-check accessibility.
6. Make sure it can be navigated using a keyboard.
7. Check to see if it works on all platforms and when projected.

For Writing for the Web

You can reach a larger audience with a simple writing style, because Web users can grasp content easily when it's clearly structured and well organized. Also, simple language helps those who are not native speakers understand the content.

With this in mind:

1. Keep your sentences short and break your text into short paragraphs.
2. Use the active voice, unless you have a good reason not to. (Say "Lee crossed a busy street." not "A busy street was crossed by Lee.")
3. Leave out needless words. Instead of: "give you notice again of the fact that" use "remind you."
4. Avoid jargon, slang, idioms, abbreviations, and acronyms, like: *FYI – he one-upped them by bugging out before they could hang him out to dry, so they were S.O.L.*

5. Define technical terms and use them as rarely as possible. For example: "Post-traumatic stress disorder (PTSD) is a type of anxiety disorder. It can occur after you've seen or experienced a traumatic event that involved the threat of injury or death."

For Design and Typography for the Web

Text is the most efficient, useful, and accessible medium for presenting information on the web, and written content is the simplest to review, search, edit, update, and correct.

To assure that your text is easy to read, use:

1. A line height between 1.3 and 1.6 em.
2. A font size between 16 px and 18 px for the body text.
3. A text width between 30 and 35 em, between 60 and 70 characters and spaces.
4. Smart quotes ‘ ’ ‘ ’ “ ” “ ” not generic quotes ' " " "
5. A smart apostrophe ’ ʼ – not a generic one ' '
6. An – en dash (– or –) with a space on either side, instead of— em dash (—) with no spaces.
7. The <em> tag for *emphasis* within a paragraph.
8. Bold and all caps, both **TOGETHER and** SEPARATELY for titles and headings only.
9. The default text property align left. Don't justify your text.
10. Make sure there is enough contrast between the text and background in menus and navigation (at least a difference of 10 in the hex colors – #000:#999, #fff:#666) and never make the text smaller than 14 px.

Tables and Lists

TABLES

HTML Elements
HTML Entities
HTML Properties
Dingbats
Block Elements
Geometric Shapes
Miscellaneous Symbols
Examples of Tables
Fractions
Using a Keyboard to Navigate Websites

LISTS

CSS Shapes
SVG Shapes

HTML Elements

Tag	Description
`<!--...-->`	Defines a comment
`<!DOCTYPE>`	Defines the document type
`<a>`	Defines a hyperlink
`<abbr>`	Defines an abbreviation
`<address>`	Defines an address element
`<area>`	Defines an area inside an image map
`<article>`	Defines an article
`<aside>`	Defines content aside from the page content

(continued)

Tag	Description
<audio>	Defines sound content
<b>	Defines bold text
<base>	Defines a base URL for all the links in a page
<bdo>	Defines the direction of text display
<blockquote>	Defines a long quotation
<body>	Defines the body element
 	Inserts a single line break
<button>	Defines a push button
<canvas>	Defines graphics
<caption>	Defines a table caption
<cite>	Defines a citation
<code>	Defines computer code text
<col>	Defines attributes for table columns
<colgroup>	Defines groups of table columns
<command>	Defines a command button
<datalist>	Defines a dropdown list
<dd>	Defines a definition description
<del>	Defines deleted text
<details>	Defines details of an element
<dfn>	Defines a definition term
<div>	Defines a section in a document
<dl>	Defines a definition list
<dt>	Defines a definition term
<em>	Defines emphasized text
<embed>	Defines external interactive content or plugin
<fieldset>	Defines a fieldset

Tag	Description
<figcaption> New	Defines the caption of a figure element
<figure>	Defines a group of media content, and their caption
<footer>	Defines a footer for a section or page
<form>	Defines a form
<h1> to <h6>	Defines header 1 to header 6
<head>	Defines information about the document
<header>	Defines a header for a section or page
<hgroup>	Defines information about a section in a document
<hr>	Defines a horizontal rule
<html>	Defines an html document
<i>	Defines italic text
<iframe>	Defines an inline sub window (frame)
<img>	Defines an image
<input>	Defines an input field
<ins>	Defines inserted text
<keygen>	Defines a generated key in a form
<kbd>	Defines keyboard text
<label>	Defines a label for a form control
<legend>	Defines a title in a fieldset
<li>	Defines a list item
<link>	Defines a resource reference
<map>	Defines an image map
<mark>	Defines marked text
<menu>	Defines a menu list
<meta>	Defines meta information
<meter>	Defines measurement within a predefined range

(continued)

Tag	Description
<nav>	Defines navigation links
<noscript>	Defines a noscript section
<object>	Defines an embedded object
<ol>	Defines an ordered list
<optgroup>	Defines an option group
<option>	Defines an option in a drop-down list
<output>	Defines some types of output
<p>	Defines a paragraph
<param>	Defines a parameter for an object
<pre>	Defines preformatted text
<progress>	Defines progress of a task of any kind
<q>	Defines a short quotation
<rt>	Defines explanation to ruby annotations
<ruby>	Defines ruby annotations
<s>	Defines text that is no longer correct
<samp>	Defines sample computer code
<script>	Defines a script
<section>	Defines a section
<select>	Defines a selectable list
<small>	Defines small text
<source>	Defines media resources
<span>	Defines a section in a document
<strike>	Not supported in HTML5
<strong>	Defines strong text
<style>	Defines a style definition
<sub>	Defines subscripted text
<summary>	Defines the header of a <detail> element

Tag	Description
<sup>	Defines superscripted text
<table>	Defines a table
<tbody>	Defines a table body
<td>	Defines a table cell
<textarea>	Defines a text area
<tfoot>	Defines a table footer
<th>	Defines a table header
<thead>	Defines a table header
<time>	Defines a date/time
<title>	Defines the document title
<tr>	Defines a table row
<ul>	Defines an unordered list
<var>	Defines a variable
<video>	Defines a video
<wbr>	Defines a possible line-break

HTML Entities – 32 to 255

Entity Name	ISO Code	Code Result	HTML Code	Code Result
space			(n/a)	(n/a)
exclamation mark	!	!	(n/a)	!
double quotes	"	"	"	"
number	#	#	(n/a)	#
dollar sign	$	$	(n/a)	$
percent	%	%	(n/a)	%
ampersand	&	&	&	&
less-than	<	<	<	<

(continued)

Entity Name	ISO Code	Code Result	HTML Code	Code Result
greater-than	>	>	>	>
vertical bar			|	(n/a)	(n/a)
function	ƒ	ƒ	(n/a)	(n/a)
double comma	„	„	(n/a)	(n/a)
ellipses	…	…	(n/a)	(n/a)
dagger	†	†	(n/a)	(n/a)
double dagger	‡	‡	(n/a)	(n/a)
circumflex	ˆ	ˆ	(n/a)	(n/a)
percentage	‰	‰	(n/a)	(n/a)
capital S hot check	Š	Š	(n/a)	(n/a)
opening quimet	‹	‹	(n/a)	(n/a)
capital O-E ligature	Œ	Œ	Œ	Œ
(n/a)		□	(n/a)	(n/a)
open single quote	‘	‘	(n/a)	(n/a)
close single quote	’	’	(n/a)	(n/a)
open double quotes	“	“	(n/a)	(n/a)
close double quotes	”	”	(n/a)	(n/a)
bullet	•	•	•	•
en dash	–	–	(n/a)	(n/a)
em dash	—	—	(n/a)	(n/a)
tilde	˜	˜	˜	˜
trademark	™	™	™	™
small s hot check	š	š	(n/a)	(n/a)
closing quimet	›	›	(n/a)	(n/a)
small o-e ligature	œ	œ	œ	Œ
Capital Y umlaut	Ÿ	Ÿ	Ÿ	Ÿ

Entity Name	ISO Code	Code Result	HTML Code	Code Result
non-breaking space				
inverted exclamation	¡	¡	¡	¡
cent	¢	¢	¢	¢
pound sterling	£	£	£	£
currency	¤	¤	¤	¤
yen	¥	¥	¥	¥
broken bar	¦	¦	&brkbar;	&brkbar;
section	§	§	§	§
umlaut (diaeresis)	¨	¨	¨	¨
copyright	©	©	©	©
feminine ordinal	ª	ª	ª	ª
left angle quote	«	«	«	«
not sign	¬	¬	¬	¬
soft hyphen				
registered	®	®	®	®
macron	¯	¯	&hibar;	&hibar;
degree	°	°	°	°
plus-minus	±	±	±	±
superscript 2	²	^{2}	²	^{2}
superscript 3	³	^{3}	³	^{3}
acute accent	´	´	´	´
micro	µ	µ	µ	µ
pilcrow	¶	¶	¶	¶
middle dot	·	·	·	·
cedilla	¸	¸	¸	¸
superscript 1	¹	^{1}	¹	^{1}

(continued)

Entity Name	ISO Code	Code Result	HTML Code	Code Result
masculine ordinal	º	º	º	º
right angle quote	»	»	»	»
one-quarter	¼	¼	¼	¼
one-half	½	½	½	½
three-quarters	¾	¾	¾	¾
inverted question mark	¿	¿	¿	¿
capital A grave	À	À	À	À
capital A acute	Á	Á	Á	Á
capital A circumflex	Â	Â	Â	Â
capital A tilde	Ã	Ã	Ã	Ã
capital A umlaut	Ä	Ä	Ä	Ä
capital A ring	Å	Å	Å	Å
capital A-E ligature	Æ	Æ	Æ	Æ
capital C cedilla	Ç	Ç	Ç	Ç
capital E grave	È	È	È	È
capital E acute	É	É	É	É
capital E circumflex	Ê	Ê	Ê	Ê
capital E umlaut	Ë	Ë	Ë	Ë
capital I grave	Ì	Ì	Ì	Ì
capital I acute	Í	Í	Í	Í
capital I circumflex	Î	Î	Î	Î
capital I umlaut	Ï	Ï	Ï	Ï
capital ETH	Ð	Ð	Ð	Ð
capital N tilde	Ñ	Ñ	Ñ	Ñ
capital O grave	Ò	Ò	Ò	Ò
capital O acute	Ó	Ó	Ó	Ó

Entity Name	ISO Code	Code Result	HTML Code	Code Result
capital O circumflex	Ô	Ô	Û	Û
capital O tilde	Õ	Õ	Õ	Õ
capital O umlaut	Ö	Ö	Ö	Ö
multiplication	×	×	×	×
capital O slash	Ø	Ø	Ø	Ø
capital U grave	Ù	Ù	Ù	Ù
capital U acute	Ú	Ú	Ã	Ã
capital U circumflex	Û	Û	Ã	Ã
capital U umlaut	Ü	Ü	Ü	Ü
capital Y acute	Ý	Ý	Ý	Ý
capital Thorn	Þ	Þ	Þ	Þ
small sharp s	ß	ß	ß	ß
small a grave	à	à	à	À
small a acute	á	á	á	Á
small a circumflex	â	â	â	Â
small a tilde	ã	ã	ã	Ã
small a umlaut	ä	ä	ä	Ä
small a ring	å	å	å	Å
small a-e ligature	æ	æ	æ	Æ
small c cedilla	ç	ç	ç	Ç
small e grave	è	è	è	È
small e acute	é	é	é	É
small e circumflex	ê	ê	ê	Ê
small e umlaut	ë	ë	ë	Ë
small i grave	ì	ì	ì	Ì
small i acute	í	í	í	Í

(continued)

Entity Name	ISO Code	Code Result	HTML Code	Code Result
small i circumflex	î	î	î	î
small i umlaut	ï	ï	ï	ï
small eth	ð	ð	ð	ð
small n tilde	ñ	ñ	ñ	ñ
small o grave	ò	ò	ò	ò
small o acute	ó	ó	ó	ó
small o circumflex	ô	ô	ô	ô
small o tilde	õ	õ	õ	õ
small o umlaut	ö	ö	ö	ö
division	÷	÷	÷	÷
small o slash	ø	ø	ø	ø
small u grave	ù	ù	ù	ù
small u acute	ú	ú	ú	ú
small u circumflex	û	û	û	û
small u umlaut	ü	ü	ü	ü
small y acute	ý	ý	ý	ý
small thorn	þ	þ	þ	þ
small y umlaut	ÿ	ÿ	ÿ	ÿ

HTML Properties

Name	Example
background	{background:#eef}
background-attachment	{background-attachment: fixed}
background-color	{background-color:#b0f505 }
background-image	{background-image:url('foo.jpg')}
background-position	{background-position:center}

Name	Example
background-repeat	{background-repeat:repeat}
border	{border:1px solid}
border-collapse	{border-collapse:collapse}
border-color	{border-color:#eed}
border-spacing	{border-spacing:10px}
border-style	{border-style:solid}
border-width	{border-width:0.3em}
bottom	{bottom:1em}
caption-side	{caption-side:bottom}
clear	{clear:both}
clip	{clip:rect(100px,150px,175px,50px)}
color	{color:#0f0}
content	{content: close-quote;}
counter-increment	{counter-increment:inherit}
counter-reset	{counter-reset:counter-name}
cursor	{cursor:crosshair}
direction	{direction:rtl}
display	{display:inline}
empty-cells	{empty-cells:show}
float	{float:right}
font	{font:15px Verdana,sans-serif}
font-family	{font-family:Georgia,Serif}
font-size	{font-size:100%}
font-style	{font-style:italic}
font-variant	{font-variant:small-caps}
font-weight	{font-weight:700}
height	{height:100px}

(continued)

Name	Example
left	{left: 2em}
letter-spacing	{letter-spacing:.02em}
line-height	{line-height: 1.5em}
list-style	{list-style:none}
list-style-image	{list-style-image:url(‹foo.gif›)}
list-style-position	{list-style-position:inside}
list-style-type	{list-style-type:upper-alpha;}
margin	{margin:1em 0.5em 1.5em}
max-height	{max-height:75%}
max-width	{max-width: 35em}
min-height	{min-height:100px}
min-width	{min-width:auto}
orphans	{orphans:3}
outline	{outline:3px solid #f90}
outline-color	{outline-color: #96f}
outline-style	{outline-style:dashed}
outline-width	{outline-width:5px}
overflow	{overflow:auto}
padding	(padding: 1em 0 1em 2em}
page-break-after	{page-break-after:always}
page-break-before	{page-break-before:auto}
page-break-inside	{page-break-inside:avoid}
position	{position:top}
quotes	{quotes:"\201c""\2 01d""\2018""\2019"}
table-layout	{table-layout:fixed}
text-align	{text-align:left}

Name	Example
text-decoration	`{text-decoration:underline}`
text-indent	`{text-indent:1em}`
text-transform	`{text-transform:small-caps}`
top	`{top:2em}`
unicode-bidi	`{unicode-bidi: embed}`
vertical-align	`{vertical-align:middle}`
visibility	`{visibility:hidden}`
white-space	`{white-space:pre-wrap}`
width	`{width:100px}`
word-spacing	`{word-spacing:.5em}`
z-index	`{z-index: auto}`

Dingbats

Character (decimal)	Decimal	Character (hex)	Hex	Name
✁	9985	✁	2701	Upper blade scissors
✂	9986	✂	2702	Black scissors
✃	9987	✃	2703	Lower blade scissors
✄	9988	✄	2704	White scissors
✆	9990	✆	2706	Telephone location sign
✇	9991	✇	2707	Tape drive
✈	9992	✈	2708	Airplane
✉	9993	✉	2709	Envelope
✌	9996	✌	270C	Victory hand
✍	9997	✍	270D	Writing hand
✎	9998	✎	270E	Lower right pencil
✏	9999	✏	270F	Pencil

(continued)

Character (decimal)	Decimal	Character (hex)	Hex	Name
✐	10000	✐	2710	Upper right pencil
✑	10001	✑	2711	White nib
✒	10002	✒	2712	Black nib
✓	10003	✓	2713	Check mark
✔	10004	✔	2714	Heavy check mark
✕	10005	✕	2715	Multiplication X
✖	10006	✖	2716	Heavy multiplication X
✗	10007	✗	2717	Ballot X
✘	10008	✘	2718	Heavy ballot X
✙	10009	✙	2719	Outlined Greek cross
✚	10010	✚	271A	Heavy Greek cross
✛	10011	✛	271B	Open center cross
✜	10012	✜	271C	Heavy open center cross
✝	10013	✝	271D	Latin cross
✞	10014	✞	271E	Shadowed white Latin cross
✟	10015	✟	271F	Outlined Latin cross
✠	10016	✠	2720	Maltese cross
✡	10017	✡	2721	Star of David
✢	10018	✢	2722	Four-teardrop-spoked asterisk
✣	10019	✣	2723	Four-balloon-spoked asterisk
✤	10020	✤	2724	Heavy four-balloon-spoked asterisk
✥	10021	✥	2725	Four-club-spoked asterisk
✦	10022	✦	2726	Black four-pointed star

Character (decimal)	Decimal	Character (hex)	Hex	Name
✧	10023	✧	2727	White four-pointed star
✩	10025	✩	2729	Stress-outlined white star
✪	10026	✪	272A	Circled white star
✫	10027	✫	272B	Open-center black star
✬	10028	✬	272C	Black-center white star
✭	10029	✭	272D	Outlined black star
✮	10030	✮	272E	Heavy outlined black star
✯	10031	✯	272F	Pinwheel star
✰	10032	✰	2730	Shadowed white star
✱	10033	✱	2731	Heavy asterisk
✲	10034	✲	2732	Open-center asterisk
✳	10035	✳	2733	Eight-spoked asterisk
✴	10036	✴	2734	Eight-pointed black star
✵	10037	✵	2735	Eight-pointed pinwheel star
✶	10038	✶	2736	Six-pointed black star
✷	10039	✷	2737	Eight-pointed rectilinear black star
✸	10040	✸	2738	Heavy eight-pointed rec-tilinear black star
✹	10041	✹	2739	Twelve-pointed black star
✺	10042	✺	273A	Sixteen-pointed asterisk
✻	10043	✻	273B	Teardrop-spoked asterisk
✼	10044	✼	273C	Open-center teardrop-spoked asterisk
✽	10045	✽	273D	Heavy teardrop-spoked asterisk

(continued)

Character (decimal)	Decimal	Character (hex)	Hex	Name
✾	10046	✾	273E	Six-petalled black & white florette
✿	10047	✿	273F	Black florette
❀	10048	❀	2740	White florette
❁	10049	❁	2741	Eight-petalled outlined black florette
❂	10050	❂	2742	Circled open-center eight- pointed star
❃	10051	❃	2743	Heavy teardrop-spoked pinwheel asterisk
❄	10052	❄	2744	Snowflake
❅	10053	❅	2745	Tight trifoliate snowflake
❆	10054	❆	2746	Heavy chevron snowflake
❇	10055	❇	2747	Sparkle
❈	10056	❈	2748	Heavy sparkle
❉	10057	❉	2749	Balloon-spoked asterisk
❊	10058	❊	274A	Eight-teardrop-spoked propeller asterisk
❋	10059	❋	274B	Heavy eight-teardrop-spoked propeller asterisk
❍	10061	❍	274D	Shadowed white circle
❏	10063	❏	274F	Lower right drop-shadowed white square
❐	10064	❐	2750	Upper right drop-shadowed white square
❑	10065	❑	2751	Lower right shadowed white square
❒	10066	❒	2752	Upper right shadowed white square

Character (decimal)	Decimal	Character (hex)	Hex	Name
❖	10070	❖	2756	Black diamond minus white X
❘	10072	❘	2758	Light vertical bar
❙	10073	❙	2759	Medium vertical bar
❚	10074	❚	275A	Heavy vertical bar
❛	10075	❛	275B	Heavy single turned comma quotation mark ornament
❜	10076	❜	275C	Heavy single comma quotation mark ornament
❝	10077	❝	275D	Heavy double turned comma quotation mark ornament
❞	10078	❞	275E	Heavy double comma quotation mark ornament
❡	10081	❡	2761	Curved stem paragraph sign ornament
❢	10082	❢	2762	Heavy exclamation mark ornament
❣	10083	❣	2763	Heavy heart exclamation mark ornament
❤	10084	❤	2764	Heavy black heart
❥	10085	❥	2765	Rotated heavy black heart bullet
❦	10086	❦	2766	Floral heart
❧	10087	❧	2767	Rotated floral heart bullet
❶	10102	❶	2776	Dingbat negative circled digit one
❷	10103	❷	2777	Dingbat negative circled digit two

(continued)

Character (decimal)	Decimal	Character (hex)	Hex	Name
❸	10104	❸	2778	Dingbat negative circled digit three
❹	10105	❹	2779	Dingbat negative circled digit four
❺	10106	❺	277A	Dingbat negative circled digit five
❻	10107	❻	277B	Dingbat negative circled digit six
❼	10108	❼	277C	Dingbat negative circled digit seven
❽	10109	❽	277D	Dingbat negative circled digit eight
❾	10110	❾	277E	Dingbat negative circled digit nine
❿	10111	❿	277F	Dingbat negative circled number ten
➀	10112	➀	2780	Dingbat circled sans-serif digit one
➁	10113	➁	2781	Dingbat circled sans-serif digit two
➂	10114	➂	2782	Dingbat circled sans-serif digit three
➃	10115	➃	2783	Dingbat circled sans-serif digit four
➄	10116	➄	2784	Dingbat circled sans-serif digit five
➅	10117	➅	2785	Dingbat circled sans-serif digit six
➆	10118	➆	2786	Dingbat circled sans-serif digit seven
➇	10119	➇	2787	Dingbat circled sans-serif digit eight

Character (decimal)	Decimal	Character (hex)	Hex	Name
➈	10120	➈	2788	Dingbat circled sans-serif digit nine
➉	10121	➉	2789	Dingbat circled sans-serif number ten
➊	10122	➊	278A	Dingbat negative circled sans-serif digit one
➋	10123	➋	278B	Dingbat negative circled sans-serif digit two
➌	10124	➌	278C	Dingbat negative circled sans-serif digit three
➍	10125	➍	278D	Dingbat negative circled sans-serif digit four
➎	10126	➎	278E	Dingbat negative circled sans-serif digit five
➏	10127	➏	278F	Dingbat negative circled sans-serif digit six
➐	10128	➐	2790	Dingbat negative circled sans-serif digit seven
➑	10129	➑	2791	Dingbat negative circled sans-serif digit eight
➒	10130	➒	2792	Dingbat negative circled sans-serif digit nine
➓	10131	➓	2793	Dingbat negative circled sans-serif number ten
➔	10132	➔	2794	Heavy wide-headed right-wards arrow
➘	10136	➘	2798	Heavy southeast arrow
➙	10137	➙	2799	Heavy rightwards arrow
➚	10138	➚	279A	Heavy northeast arrow
➛	10139	➛	279B	Drafting pointT right-wards arrow

(continued)

Character (decimal)	Decimal	Character (hex)	Hex	Name
➜	10140	➜	279C	Heavy round-tipped rightwards arrow
➝	10141	➝	279D	Triangle-headed rightwards arrow
➞	10142	➞	279E	Heavy triangle-headed rightwards arrow
➟	10143	➟	279F	Dashed triangle-headed rightwards arrow
➠	10144	➠	27A0	Heavy dashed triangle-headed rightwards arrow
➡	10145	➡	27A1	Black rightwards arrow
➢	10146	➢	27A2	Three-D top-lighted rightwards arrowhead
➣	10147	➣	27A3	Three-D bottom-lighted rightwards arrowhead
➤	10148	➤	27A4	Black rightwards arrowhead
➥	10149	➥	27A5	Heavy black curved downwards & rightwards arrow
➦	10150	➦	27A6	Heavy black curved upwards & rightwards arrow
➧	10151	➧	27A7	Squat T black rightwards arrow
➨	10152	➨	27A8	Heavy concave-pointed black rightwards arrow
➩	10153	➩	27A9	Right-shaded white rightwards arrow
➪	10154	➪	27AA	Left-shaded white rightwards arrow

Character (decimal)	Decimal	Character (hex)	Hex	Name
➫	10155	➫	27AB	Back-tilted shadowed white rightwards arrow
➬	10156	➬	27AC	Front-titled shadowed white rightwards arrow
➭	10157	➭	27AD	Heavy lower right-shadowed white rightwards arrow
➮	10158	➮	27AE	Heavy upper right-shadowed white rightwards arrow
➯	10159	➯	27AF	Notched lower right-shadowed white rightwards arrow
➱	10161	➱	27B1	Notched upper right-shadowed white rightwards arrow
➲	10162	➲	27B2	Circled heavy white rightwards arrow
➳	10163	➳	27B3	White-feathered rightwards arrow
➴	10164	➴	27B4	Black-feathered southeast arrow
➵	10165	➵	27B5	Black-feathered rightwards arrow
➶	10166	➶	27B6	Black-feathered northeast arrow
➷	10167	➷	27B7	Heavy black-feathered southeast arrow
➸	10168	➸	27B8	Heavy black-feathered rightwards arrow
➹	10169	➹	27B9	Heavy black-feathered northeast arrow

(continued)

Character (decimal)	Decimal	Character (hex)	Hex	Name
➺	10170	➺	27BA	Teardrop-barbed rightwards arrow
➻	10171	➻	27BB	Heavy teardrop-shanked rightwards arrow
➼	10172	➼	27BC	Wedge-tailed rightwards arrow
➽	10173	➽	27BD	Heavy wedge-tailed rightwards arrow
➾	10174	➾	27BE	Open-outlined rightwards arrow

Block Elements

Character (decimal)	Decimal	Character (hex)	Hex	Name
▁	9601	▁	2581	Lower ⅛ block
▂	9602	▂	2582	Lower ¼ block
▃	9603	▃	2583	Lower ⅜ block
▄	9604	▄	2584	Lower ½ block
▅	9605	▅	2585	Lower ⅝ block
▆	9606	▆	2586	Lower ⅝ block
▇	9607	▇	2587	Lower ⅞ block
█	9608	█	2588	Full block
▉	9609	▉	2589	Left ⅞ block
▊	9610	▊	258A	Left ¾ block
▋	9611	▋	258B	Left ⅝ block
▌	9612	▌	258C	Left ½ block
▍	9613	▍	258D	Left ⅜ block
▎	9614	▎	258E	Left ¼ block

Character (decimal)	Decimal	Character (hex)	Hex	Name
▏	9615	▏	258F	Left ⅛ block
▒	9618	▒	2592	Medium shade
▓	9619	▓	2593	Dark shade
▔	9620	▔	2594	Upper ⅛ block
▕	9621	▕	2595	Right ⅛ block

Geometric Shapes

Character (decimal)	Decimal	Character (hex)	Hex	Name
■	9632	■	25A0	Black square
□	9633	□	25A1	White square
▣	9635	▣	25A3	White square containing black small square
▤	9636	▤	25A4	Square with horizontal fill
▥	9637	▥	25A5	Square with vertical fill
▦	9638	▦	25A6	Square with orthogonal crosshatch fill
▧	9639	▧	25A7	Square with upper left to lower right fill
▨	9640	▨	25A8	Square with upper right to lower left fill
▩	9641	▩	25A9	Square with diagonal crosshatch fill
▪	9642	▪	25AA	Black small square
▲	9650	▲	25B2	Black up-pointing triangle
△	9651	△	25B3	White up-pointing triangle

(continued)

Character (decimal)	Decimal	Character (hex)	Hex	Name
▶	9654	▶	25B6	Black right-pointing triangle
▷	9655	▷	25B7	White right-pointing triangle
▼	9660	▼	25BC	Black down-pointing triangle
▽	9661	▽	25BD	White down-pointing triangle
◀	9664	◀	25C0	Black left-pointing triangle
◁	9665	◁	25C1	White left-pointing triangle
◆	9670	◆	25C6	Black diamond
◇	9671	◇	25C7	White diamond
◈	9672	◈	25C8	White diamond containing black small diamond
◊	9674	◊	25CA	Lozenge
○	9675	○	25CB	White circle
◌	9676	◌	25CC	Dotted circle
◎	9678	◎	25CE	Bulls eye
●	9679	●	25CF	Black circle
◐	9680	◐	25D0	Circle with left half black
◑	9681	◑	25D1	Circle with right half black
◢	9698	◢	25E2	Black lower right triangle
◣	9699	◣	25E3	Black lower left triangle

Character (decimal)	Decimal	Character (hex)	Hex	Name
◤	9700	◤	25E4	Black upper left triangle
◥	9701	◥	25E5	Black upper right triangle
◦	9702	◦	25E6	White bullet
◯	9711	◯	25EF	Large circle

Miscellaneous Symbols

Character (decimal)	Decimal	Character (hex)	Hex	Name
★	9733	★	2605	Black star
☆	9734	☆	2606	White star
☎	9742	☎	260E	Black telephone
☏	9743	☏	260F	White telephone
☜	9756	☜	261C	White left pointing index
☞	9758	☞	261E	White right pointing index
♀	9792	♀	2640	Female sign
♂	9794	♂	2642	Male sign
♔	9812	♔	2654	White chess king
♕	9813	♕	2655	White chess queen
♖	9814	♖	2656	White chess rook
♗	9815	♗	2657	White chess bishop
♘	9816	♘	2658	White chess knight
♙	9817	♙	2659	White chess pawn

(continued)

Character (decimal)	Decimal	Character (hex)	Hex	Name
♚	9818	♚	265A	Black chess king
♛	9819	♛	265B	Black chess queen
♜	9820	♜	265C	Black chess rook
♝	9821	♝	265D	Black chess bishop
♞	9822	♞	265E	Black chess knight
♟	9823	♟	265F	Black chess pawn
♠	9824	♠	2660	Black spade suit
♡	9825	♡	2661	White heart suit
♢	9826	♢	2662	White diamond suit
♣	9827	♣	2663	Black club suit
♤	9828	♤	2664	White spade suit
♥	9829	♥	2665	Black heart suit
♦	9830	♦	2666	Black diamond suit
♧	9831	♧	2667	White club suit
♨	9832	♨	2668	Hot springs
♩	9833	♩	2669	Quarter note
♪	9834	♪	266A	Eighth note
♬	9836	♬	266C	Beamed sixteenth notes
♭	9837	♭	266D	Music flat sign
♯	9839	♯	266F	Music sharp sign
⚀	9856	⚀	2680	Die face-1
⚁	9857	⚁	2681	Die face-2
⚂	9858	⚂	2682	Die face-3
⚃	9859	⚃	2683	Die face-4
⚄	9860	⚄	2684	Die face-5
⚅	9861	⚅	2685	Die face-6

Examples ofTables

Information about Selected Individuals

Name	Address	Phone	Email	Age	Occupation
Jerome Murray	495 East Pine Grove Road, Pennsylvania Furnace, PA 16867	(814) 237-2138	jbm282@psu.edu	76	Retired plumber
Alfred Murray	2111 Oxford Place, Lexington, KY 40661	(502) 352-1326	awm500@gmail.com	34	Kentucky State employee
Mary Anne Wilson	495 East Pine Grove Road, PA Furnace, PA 16867	(814) 237-2138	mawilson@aol.com	73	Social worker
Joan Bernheimer	170 E 86St, Indianapolis, IN 46244	(317) 271-6879	jaz81819@aol.com	79	Retired teacher
Gillian Norris	812 Fare St, Apt 32, Cambridge, MA 02238	(617) 791-4973	None	50	Librarian
Albert Minton	2111 London Lane, Lexington, MA 00661	(502) 352-1326	minton8@gmail.com	24	Waiter
Charles Tryon	4222 Arlington Ave, Ft Wayne, IN 46900	(307) 243-3451	cxt349@iu.edu	41	Insurance salesman

Different formats and abbreviations.				
25-Aug-12	25.8.12	August 25, 2012	8/25/2012	
9.98	$9.98	12 pounds 54 pence	£12.54	**£12.54**
15 euros 63 cents	€15.63	43 Yen	¥43	

(continued)

Different formats and abbreviations.				
2 pounds 3 ounces	2 lbs 3 oz	6 kilograms	6 kilos	6 kg
abbr	Ave. Ave	Assn. Assn	10 km	Ltd. Ltd
10 mph	10 mm	St. St	Corp. Corp	dept. dept
dist. dist	div. div	Dr. Dr	est. est	et al.
pl. pl	ft. ft	gal. gal	Gov. Gov	Inc. Inc

NEDA Eating Disorders
Men and women are subject to eating disorders on campuses across the nation. Most colleges recognize the issue, but only 58% consider eating disorders "very important."
4–10% of men on college campuses have eating disorders.
10–20% of women on college campuses have eating disorders.
35% of normal "dieters" progress to pathological dieting.
20–25% of normal "dieters" progress to partial or full-syndrome eating disorders.
73% of colleges participate in NEDA awareness week activities.
94.1% of respondents said that eating disorders are important.
36% of respondents said that eating disorders are somewhat important.
60% of respondents said that eating disorders are very/extremely important.

Fractions

These codes allow fractions to be represented with typographically smaller numerators and denominators.

Character Name	Character	Entity	Num Entity	Hex Entity
Vulgar fraction 1/4	¼	¼	¼	¼
Vulgar fraction 1/2	½	½	½	½

Character Name	Character	Entity	Num Entity	Hex Entity
Vulgar fraction 3/4	¾	¾	¾	¾
Vulgar fraction 1/3	⅓	–	⅓	⅓
Vulgar fraction 2/3	⅔	–	⅔	⅔
Vulgar fraction 1/5	⅕	–	⅕	⅕
Vulgar fraction 2/5	⅖	–	₢	⅖
Vulgar fraction 3/5	⅗	–	⅗	⅗
Vulgar fraction 4/5	⅘	–	⅘	⅘
Vulgar fraction 1/6	⅙	–	⅙	⅙
Vulgar fraction 5/6	⅚	–	⅚	⅚
Vulgar fraction 1/8	⅛	–	⅛	⅛
Vulgar fraction 3/8	⅜	–	⅜	⅜
Vulgar fraction 5/8	⅝	–	⅝	⅝
Vulgar fraction 7/8	⅞	–	⅞	⅞

Using a Keyboard to Navigate Websites

These common keyboard commands can be used to navigate the web without a mouse.

If you want to –	Select
Forward from link to link or to controls	Tab
Backward from link to link or to controls	Shift + Tab
Select buttons	Spacebar
Navigate and select radio buttons	Arrow
Select/deselect boxes	Spacebar
Move from box to box	Tab
Open a list box	ALT + Down arrow

(continued)

If you want to –	Select
Read the prior screen	CTRL(⌘) + Page Up
Read the next screen	CTRL(⌘) + Page Down
Go to the top of the page	CTRL(⌘) + Up arrow
Go to the bottom of the page	CTRL(⌘) + Down arrow
Refresh the screen	F5
Go back a page	ALT + Left Arrow
Go forward a page	ALT + Right Arrow
Highlight URL in address bar	CTRL(⌘) + L
Hide a page	CTRL(⌘) + H
Copy selected text	CTRL(⌘) + C
Paste selected text	CTRL(⌘) + V

CSS Shapes

These are shapes that can be included in a web page by adding the markup to your style sheet and your web page. Size, border and color can be changed in the markup.

Square

```
#square{width:100px;height:100px;background#000;}
```

Rectangle

```
#rectangle{width:200px;height:100px;background:#000;}
```

Circle

```
#circle{width:100px;height:100px;background:#000;-moz-border-
radius:50px;-webkit-border-radius:50px;border-radius:50px;}
```

Oval

```
#oval{width:200px;height:100px;background:#000;-moz-border-
radius:100px/50px;-webkit-border-radius:100px/50px;border-
radius:100px/50px;}
```

Triangle Up

```
#triangle-up{width:0;height:0;border-left:50px solid transparent;
border-right:50px solid transparent;border-bottom:100px solid
#000;}
```

Triangle Down

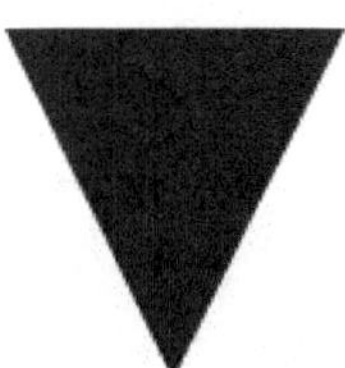

```
#triangle-down{width:0;height:0;border-left:50px solid transparent;
border-right:50px solid transparent;border-top:100px solid #000;}
```

Triangle Left

```
#triangle-left{width:0;height:0;border-top:50px solid transparent;
border-right:100px solid #000;border-bottom:50px solid transparent;}
```

Triangle Right

```
#s#triangle-right{width:0;height:0;border-top:50px solid transparent;
border-left:100px solid #000;border-bottom:50px solid transparent;}
```

Trapezoid

```
#trapezoid{border-bottom:100px solid #000;border-left:50px solid
transparent;border-right:50px solid transparent;height:0;width:
100px;}
```

Parallelogram

```
#parallelogram{width:150px;height:100px;-webkit-transform:skew
(20deg);-moz-transform:skew(20deg);-o-transform:skew(20deg);
background:#000;}
```

SVG Shapes

These are shapes that can be included in a web page by adding the markup to your style sheet and your web page. Size, border, color and opacity can be changed in the markup.

Square

```
rect fill="#000"x="0"y="10"width="100"height="100"
```

Circle

```
circle fill="#000" cx="50" cy="50" r="50"
```

Triangle

```
path fill="000" d="m 50 10 l 50 100 -100 0 z" /
```

Triangle at a slant

```
path fill="000" d="m 50 10 l 150 100 -100 0 z" /
```

Rectangle

```
rect fill="#000" x="110" y="10" width="80" height="80" /
```

The following commands are for path data:

M = moveto
L = lineto
H = horizontal lineto
V = vertical lineto
C = curveto
S = smooth curveto
Q = quadratic Bézier curve
T = smooth quadratic Bézier curveto
A = elliptical Arc
Z = closepath